LIFE ENHANCEMENT WITH *Jesus*

THE WITNESS OF ONE ORDINARY MAN

LIFE
ENHANCEMENT
WITH *Jesus*

THE WITNESS OF ONE ORDINARY MAN

JIM BRANDT

LitPrime
"Your story is our priority"

LitPrime Solutions
21250 Hawthorne Blvd
Suite 500, Torrance, CA 90503
www.litprime.com
Phone: 1-800-981-9893

Published by LitPrime Solutions   01/06/2023

ISBN: 979-8-88703-107-1(sc)
ISBN: 979-8-88703-108-8(e)

Library of Congress Control Number: 2022922749

To

My children, Jessica (the editor of this book) and Nathan, who were the original reason I wrote the book. Both made my life special.

My wife Charity helped me during my effort to focus on creating meaning for my life.

My sister Edna and her husband Bill were always there for me. They put the needs of others ahead of their challenges.

My Mother and Father. My mother always put my sister and me first. My father was the most significant role model I ever met. He was there for everyone.

Pastor Mu helped me to see how I could come from a different church and grow my faith in his church. He respects that I see my relationship with Jesus as an essential objective.

James Barber helped me understand critical spiritual concepts through his teaching at the Sabbath School. He was never judgmental.

All the Elders and members of the New Life Seventh Day Adventist Church helped me to understand the connection between my life experiences and my faith.

CONTENTS

INTRODUCTION

M y purpose in writing this book is in three parts. First, I want to communicate to my children how my faith in God has helped my life and the lives of people around me. Second to show my wife Charity how she helped me understand how my faith affected my life. The third purpose is to be a witness of how faith in God has directly affected my life. My witness is an account without listing scripture. I am not a Biblical Scholar; I am a regular person who is lucky to have the right family, a great wife (Charity), and good friends who helped me.

The content of this book is limited to those facts that lead me to grow my faith in God. Details about my accomplishments are not included to avoid distractions.

I was blessed to have exciting experiences at an early age that allowed me to accept that the Bible is true; freeing me to spend time working to understand how the word of God improves our lives. However, I strayed from the principles of Christianity many times during my life. If at an early age, I realized the effect Christian principles had on my life, I would be better. I hope those who read this book understand that concept much earlier in their lives than I did.

I grew up as a Christian. My mother's family was Presbyterian, and my father's family was Baptist.

Although I attended church regularly when I was growing up, I was not as consistent as an adult. I always had faith, but sometimes, I let other priorities prevail. It was not until much later in my life that I began to see how critical my faith was.

I had many experiences during my life that helped me feel close to God, but I did not understand the effect of God until much later. Earlier, I was more concerned with advancing my own life than by living within Christian values. Promoting my personal life made my development much more difficult, but gratefully, the meaning of the Christian experiences became clear. I received guidance from several role models, but I did not realize it was their guidance I was following.

When my children were living with me, I kept my Christian values to myself. Their mother did not believe in God, so I was careful not to pray in front of the children, but I did take them to church occasionally. Their mother did not interfere with my Christianity, but I was not comfortable praying in front of everyone. Also, I was taught in Sunday School to pray in private. I should pray about personal topics in private, but I should pray with my children for meals, trips, etc.

Hopefully, many of you who read this book will understand the importance of living up to your Christian values much sooner than I did.

CHAPTER 1

THE BEGINNING

I was born on May 10, 1950, in a very small town called Hayfork. Hayfork was in the mountains of Northern California. There was no hospital, so my mother had to go to a doctor's office to give birth.

Family Structure

My father left my mother when I was only one year old. My mother remarried when I was a little over two years old. My mother's new husband adopted me, so I have his last name. I will refer to my mother's second husband as my father during the remainder of this book. He was the greatest asset to growing my faith. He truly lived Christian values, even when it was difficult for him.

My mother was a good Christian. Her strength was how much she loved her family and the sacrifices she made without any regrets.

I have a sister who is two years younger than me. She shares our Christian values. She and I were Baptized together when I was in high school. Our baptism was a major event. Our entire family supported it.

Our family moved several times before my graduation from high school. That meant we changed churches several times. My father made it clear that it was not that important which church we attended

1

because our faith was personal with God. The church provided a place to pay respect to God, a place to meet people with similar beliefs, and a place to learn more about the Bible. Our family did not worry about rules and guidelines that were specific to a Church unless those rules were part of overall scripture teachings.

Most of the family on my father's side lived in Redding, California (Northern California). I had two aunts, two uncles, grandfather, grandmother, and many cousins. They all belonged to the Redding First Baptist Church. My grandmother also taught Sunday School at a tiny one-room church that was in their neighborhood. My sister and I attended the local one-room church when we were very young. My grandparents on my mother's side of the family lived in the town where I was born, Hayfork (about a two-hour drive from Redding at that time). My mother also had a sister who lived in Redding.

During several summers in the late 1950s and early 1960s, my sister and I spent two weeks in Redding at my father's parent's house and two weeks in Hayfork at my mother's parent's house. We did attend church regularly in Redding, and only a couple of times in Hayfork.

My Mother and Father

My Sister Edna and Me

First Vision

I was six years old. My sister and I went to Hayfork to visit our Grandparents. Hayfork was a tiny town up in the mountains. We went to Sunday School that day at my grandparent's church. We played near my grandparent's horses.

That night we asked my grandfather if we could sleep outside in their travel trailer. My grandfather said we could if the dog slept with us.

During the night, I had a dream I can still remember to this day. After I fell asleep, I was on a beach next to the ocean. There were lots of people on the beach and in the water.

Suddenly, I heard bolts of lightning. I looked up in the sky, and I felt the beach shake. I saw four lightning bolts, one from each corner of the sky streaking to the center of the air. When the four lightning bolts met, there was a small space between the ends of the four streaks of lightning.

Then there was a man inside the rectangle dressed in a white robe off in the distance. Then the man moved closer, and I could see it was Jesus. I had just seen a picture showing Jesus in Sunday School that morning. I could see Jesus lift his arms. People from under the beach rose to the sky. Then another group of people began to rise.

Jesus In the Distant Sky with Lightning

My grandfather entered the trailer and woke me up. He said that a cow escaped from a neighbor's property and the cow was banging into the travel trailer. I told my grandfather about the dream. He felt it was a combination of the cow bumping into the travel trailer and the Sunday School lesson I had earlier.

My grandfather's explanation seemed logical, but years later, I began to think about it.

Long after I became an adult, I realized the vision was showing me the second coming of Jesus.

Although initially, I did not realize how important this dream was, I never doubted Jesus was truly the Savior. I questioned many concepts from the Church, but never questioned the fact Jesus did come to Earth, he was crucified, and he will come back. What an advantage this was because I did spend time wondering what scriptures meant; which ones were symbols or parables and which ones were literal. But knowing that Jesus is the Savior makes everything else different.

However, it was not for many years that I looked back on the dream of Jesus and realized three very important points. First, I had never seen a beach before that dream. This was before television, so I had never seen one. How did I know I was at a beach? I can still remember standing on the sand seeing people talking with each other while others were rising through the sand.

The second point is that I was not taught about Jesus's second coming until many years later. At that time, I was taught you went straight to Heaven when you died. Yet in the dream, I saw people who I knew had died rise through the sand when Jesus raised his arms.

The third point is that in the dream Jesus never touched the earth. I did not know this point was significant until just a few months ago when I learned from scripture that Jesus will not touch the earth when he returns.

Since I was only six years old at the time, I understand that I did not think about these three points. However, later these points were major contributors to strengthening my faith.

CHAPTER 2

EARLY YEARS

When I was twelve years old, my father made an unselfish decision that affected my entire life. He moved our family to Paradise, California. He did this even though it meant he would have to commute fifty miles to work each way.

Paradise was a beautiful town, especially back when I lived there. It was tiny, only 5 thousand people. It was up in the mountains with lots of pine trees. Our family loved living there.

I was active in the Boy Scouts; my father was an Eagle Scout. He was involved in my Boy Scout troop. Our family attended the First Baptist Church in Paradise. The church did not have its building, but the Seventh Day Adventist Church allowed our church to worship in their church on Sundays since their day of worship was Saturday. My father and I worked on the weekends to help our church build its facility over two years. I would go to the Seventh Day Adventist Church early every Sunday morning and replace all the songbooks, put up signs, and place the programs in designated areas. I would return everything after the service.

My early years went well. My father worked for the State of California as a civil engineer, and my mother was a waitress at several different restaurants. I was competitive at school, both with academics and sports. I had challenges during the early years, but by the early 1960's I developed in both areas. My parents had financial difficulties at that time, but I did not know the difference. They took excellent care of my sister and me, always putting our needs first.

At that time, Paradise had three main religions: Protestants, Catholics, and Mormons. The Catholics and Mormons had their schools from grades 1 through 8. Beyond the eighth grade, everyone was in the same school. It was a challenging experience to socialize among the three groups. I learned how to be tolerant of other people's religions and views. At that time Protestants did not socialize with Catholics, at least not in Paradise. That made the experience to socialize with people from other religions even better.

I advanced in sports and academics. Everything was going well.

Taken One Month Before I Left Paradise

Second Vision

In the middle of my junior year in high school, in 1967, everything changed. My father was transferred to Southern California to complete the State Water Project.

I was devastated. I tried to create a plan so I could live with my best friend, Ray Humphrey, but after much discussion, my father said no. He said I had to move. I became very depressed. I knew I would not be competitive in sports after the move because the competition was so much better in Los Angeles. I was concerned about academics as well. I was doing so well, and I did not wish to start over somewhere new halfway through my junior year in high school.

I loved living in Paradise and did not think I would ever be happy again. I remember my last day in Paradise. I had a 1954 Ford Pickup I purchased several months earlier. I drove it to a service station for a tune-up so it would be ready for the trip to Los Angeles the next day. I was walking by myself along the main road called "Billie Road." I was so depressed thinking that my life would never be as good as it was the last six years.

Then for some reason, I asked God to help me. I did not bow my head to pray. I just started talking. I asked for help to stay in Paradise. As I kept walking, I started feeling a vision of opportunity. The feeling was inside me, but I did not see anything. I started imagining good possibilities. Almost immediately, Southern California did not seem so bad. I began to feel the energy, thinking about the opportunity to experience a completely different life. The feeling was a surprise because I never wanted to travel anywhere because I was so happy where I was.

I had a strong feeling that I would grow substantially after the move because of all the new experiences. Instead of worrying about being able to stay in Paradise, I began to think about the opportunity to meet new people and learn from more advanced schools. I was still nervous about being able to compete, but I was open to the chance to try.

It was February of my Junior Year in High School. That meant I had already played football that year and half of the wrestling season. I knew my sports opportunity was over, but I thought I could work hard and grow much more academically than I would have in Paradise.

I was not happy, but by the time I retrieved my truck from the service station and began to drive home for the last time, I felt the challenge, and I did have confidence. I felt much better the next morning when I prepared to begin the ten-hour trip. My mother and sister went into my mother's car, and I followed in my truck.

The trip down to Los Angeles was not depressing. I think the challenge of driving to so many new places was exiting since before the trip to Los Angeles, I had not driven more than two hours from home.

The big challenge came near the end of the trip when a police officer signaled me to stop. He did not give me a ticket; he stopped me because I was driving too slowly. At that time, I had little experience driving on freeways.

CHAPTER 3

FINISHING HIGH SCHOOL

For the first month after arriving in Southern California, we lived in a motel. I drove my truck to school. It did not take long to learn how to drive on the freeways.

I was nervous for the first couple of days at school. The quality of education was much better than in Paradise, which meant there were more challenges to succeed. I met several of the students on the first day. That made the time at school more comfortable.

My initial experience with the sports program was much better than even the vision I had that last day in Paradise. I met one of the school's best athletes on the first day. Within a few days, we became good friends. He introduced me to the track coach the next day.

Within two weeks, I had completely changed my approach to high jumping. I was the top high jumper in the school within three weeks. At Paradise, my best performance as a high jumper was 5 feet, 6 inches. I cleared 5 feet, 10 inches by the second week and six feet three inches by the end of the year. That was substantially above the school record in Paradise.

I remember I thought the reason I did so well was because of the coaching, but if that was the reason, why is it that no one else was performing as well?

During my senior year, I was on the football team, wrestling team, and track team. I was very successful in all three sports and later attended college with a full football scholarship. By the end of my senior year, I knew the move from Paradise opened a lot of opportunities in my life. My vision the last day in Paradise walking along Billie Road made sense to me. That was the first time I realized that sometimes when things look bad, after time passes, the outcome seems much different. I learned to wait for a while before judging the value of a situation.

Relationship with My Birth Father

My mother told me a little bit about my birth father, and she did allow me to see him a few times as I grew up. However, my grandmother on my mother's side made it clear my birth father was an evil person, and I should not spend time thinking about him. From the time I was five years old, I heard my birth father was an alcoholic and had no redeeming value.

During that time, I did not question things. I did see my birth father five or six times as I grew up. My mother and father would cooperate with him and make it easy for me to spend some time with him. Many years later, I was very grateful I spent that time with him.

Because of the input from my grandparents, I never allowed myself to be close to my birth father. Many years later, I regretted allowing my grandmother to have that much influence.

He was always lovely, but I never really knew him. I made no effort to learn who he was. When he tried to reach me after I moved to Southern California, I ignored him because of what my grandmother told me.

Many years later, I was devastated by my actions. I wanted to reverse everything, but it was too late. Then I studied the Sermon on the Mount. During that message, Jesus taught me how to manage precisely situations like the one with my birth father. When I reviewed the Sermon, I thought about how I judged my father. I wish I asked him about his life and learned for myself. He approached me when I was a senior in high school. I was old enough to know better, but I did not see how important it was to meet with him and learn about his challenges.

Five years later, I felt the worst pain I ever felt because I did not allow him to tell me his story. I will address what happened in Chapter 5 – Marine Corps.

High School Sports in Southern California

I began in February of 1967, halfway through my junior year in high school. When I think back on it, I adjusted to the new life immediately. I began several friendships the first day and continued to develop more as time passed.

The two most prominent friends I met were the star football player and a girl who later became my wife. The star football player named Casey was the best athlete in the school. He played football, basketball, and was on the track team. I spent many nights at his house, and we eventually became roommates in college. He helped me compete in sports in Southern California. He had amazing self-confidence.

I believe my relationship with Casey helped me create close relationships with many others in the sports program.

One aspect of the vision I had in Paradise that last day was sports. I felt a strong sense that athletics would become much more critical to my growth in Southern California than in Paradise. However, that last day in Paradise, I did not have confidence I could compete in Southern California, let alone be successful.

The last church I attended in Paradise was the First Baptist Church. During the second half of high school and college, I rarely attended church and did not pray as often. I still had strong feelings inside about how I should live, especially when I was considering doing something that I knew was wrong.

I am not sure how much it hurt not to attend church during those years. I still had faith God was the Creator, and Jesus will come, but I did not make that faith the driving part of my life.

However, the vision from the last day in Paradise became more real than I ever imagined possible.

Now I know my faith was the driving force, even when I did not follow the message from the vision. After I finished a very successful track season, school ended for that year. My mother was able to get me a job at the restaurant where she worked. I liked the people working at the restaurant, and I learned a lot about the restaurant business. I also enjoyed the additional income.

The work was going so well, I decided not to play football my senior year.

At that time, I did not see how much participation in sports would lead to valuable opportunities. I saw that if I did not play football, I would have more money and freedom. I would not have to practice every day, and I would earn the income to have more freedom. I realized it was the right decision.

So, I did not report to football practice near the end of the summer. My new friends were surprised, but they did not know how insecure I felt about sports at that time. Everything was going well at work, and I enjoyed the freedom of having money.

I did talk to the players on the football team. They seemed very happy. Then a key player was hurt and would not be able to play the rest of the season. The football coach asked me to meet him in his office at school. He told me I was short-sided and made the wrong decision not to play football. I listened to him, but my thoughts were that he did not know me or what my future would be. How could he possibly be able to give me good advice? I did tell him I would think about it.

I was sure I would keep working and adjust my life accordingly. Then I had a dream that night that stuck with me for the rest of my life. I was playing football. I was struggling as I expected. I was trying as hard as I could and did not have the skills required to be successful. Then later in the dream, I changed my goals; <u>instead of working as hard as I could to be a good football player, I focused all my energy on helping the team play better</u>. It was a fantastic feeling. I did not care how well I played, but I did care about how much I contributed.

The next morning, I told my mother I would no longer attend work. I told her I would call the manager that morning and let him know I was resigning immediately. That was a difficult call, but the manager understood.

As soon as I arrived at school, I went to the coach's office and let him know I decided to play. He immediately went with me to the locker room and gave me the equipment I needed. I went to practice that day and bonded quickly with the team.

After the first practice, I knew I made the best decision and never thought about not playing again. The other players noticed my attitude about playing for the team, not myself. It was apparent I was not working to make myself look good, but I was working very hard to help the team. I was shocked at how quickly everyone noticed that change.

That lesson of putting the team first helped me excel with wrestling and track. By the end of the year, I had football college scholarship offers and had earned the respect of the school even though I was only there one full year.

In the end, I did play football one year at a junior college because, at that time, the NCAA did not allow first-year students in college to play varsity sports. I did play college football beginning my sophomore year with a full scholarship.

Again, at that time, I did not understand it was my faith in God that allowed me to see the better approach to the game. It was not until many years later that I looked back on those days and saw the connection between the dream and the new contributions I made to the team. Then I would learn how this lesson of working to help the team helped me with many future relationships and challenges.

Dating to Marriage

During my first day of school in Southern California, I met a person in two of my classes: History and Speech. I thought she was in her junior year as I was because we were in the same history class. However, later, I learned she was in her senior year because she transferred from Pennsylvania, where history was not a junior year class. I was surprised when she told me she was a senior, but it did not influence the relationship.

She was the most intelligent student in the school, but she did not have the highest grade-point average. The school she attended in Pennsylvania was much more challenging to earn higher grades. So, her grade-point average was lower than it would have been in California.

I started dating her by the end of the first week. My life ambition was to be a U.S. Senator. At first, I was attracted to her because she was so smart, but later I saw much more in her.

She was participating in a speech contest. I was able to attend some of her speeches. She was impressive. I enjoyed the time we spent together. She only had one semester left before she left for college. After she left for college, we only spent time together a few times a year. However, the relationship did continue to grow.

As the relationship developed, we discussed the topic of religion. I realized she was agnostic, but she did attend an agnostic church. She seemed to have Christian values such as extreme honesty, concern for others and putting other's needs in front of her own. But there was another side to her. She was very critical of others and did not hesitate to let them know. Some of my new friends were surprised I was dating her. They all avoided her because of the way she verbally attacked them. She was not afraid to take anyone to task. She was very confident in her analytical skills.

One of my new friends, who was President of the Senior Class and a star on the football team, told me I was not very smart for dating her. He told me how she put him down in front of an entire lunch crowd because there was trash in the senior square during lunch. He cleaned all the debris.

I saw a different side of her. She cared very much about other people and supported them in many ways. She had friends who understood her and enjoyed spending time with her.

First Near-Death Experience

During the time we were dating, I purchased a motorcycle. I loved riding it. California had not passed the law to require motorcycle drivers to wear a helmet. I never wore a helmet. However, my girlfriend's father insisted she wear a helmet while riding on the motorcycle. She usually kept her helmet at her house. However, she left the helmet at my home after my parents hosted a party for the football team. The next morning when I was going to meet her, I wore her helmet because it was too difficult to carry it while I was riding on the motorcycle. While driving up the on-ramp to the freeway, a truck hit the motorcycle and knocked it down. The trailer of the truck drove over my head and left a tread mark on the helmet. I only had minor injuries, but I knew it could have been much worse. God protected me even when I did not think I needed protecting. I had motorcycles for the next forty-five years, and I always wore a helmet.

My First Wife's Family

Her family was very educated. Her brother attended Brown University for his undergraduate degree, and he earned his Ph.D. in Astro Physics at Harvard. He was a rocket scientist at NASA. He was the smartest person I ever met. During the summer following my junior year in high school, I spent a good part of my time with him. He was terrific. We went on hikes in the local mountains, swam at the beach, and watched sporting events. I liked him, and of course, I was impressed with his ability to analyze everything.

My girlfriend left for college at the University of California at Santa Barbara. It was only a ninety-minute drive to visit her, so I made the trip when I could. That year was hectic for me because I was working hard with sports while seeking a college scholarship, working part-time, and doing my best to excel in school.

Her parents made it clear they did not favor the relationship. The next morning after we had been on a date, her father called my father and told him I was not to see her again. My father told him he did not have control over the way I spent my time. I did not even live at home at that point.

We continued to see each other without her parent's knowledge. It made things difficult when she was home on break, but we managed.

CHAPTER 4

COLLEGE YEARS

Challenges with the New Relationship

When looking back on that first year of college, as you would expect, her parent's expressions against our relationship made us closer.

Her major in college was Russian. She did so well that she was selected to go to Russia for a year on an exchange program. Being selected was a significant achievement for her, but it was a source of tension for me.

I wanted her to experience the highest levels of success. The challenge for me was that it was 1968, the Vietnam War was in progress, and the Military Draft had begun. I registered for the draft. After the draft lottery, I would serve in the military (my draft number was low). It was tough for me to think about going to fight a war and my future wife living in the country that was supporting the enemy.

However, I did not know what to do.

After about a week, I felt some clarity. I would not make any ultimatums but would express my challenges. I let her know how proud I was she was chosen to represent the United States in the program and that I wanted her to achieve her dreams.

I also expressed my negative feelings about the Russian government and their support for the North Vietnamese. However, based on the feelings I had during my prayers; I made no demands. I made it clear that if she decided to go to Russia, that decision would not end our relationship.

I prayed often trying to verify I did not put too much pressure on her but did communicate my thoughts.

She decided to think about it for a couple of weeks. The University of Leningrad did not require a decision for about six weeks. I felt OK when she told me.

I prayed many more times about the situation. The plan did not change. I just left the decision to her and did my best to be supportive if she chose to go to Russia.

At that time, I was communicating with different universities regarding football scholarships. I had several offers. I waited until she made her decision, then I decided which college.

She decided not to go to Russia. I was happy at first, but then I realized I was the reason she did not reach her dream. That fact would burden me heavily for most of my life. To this day, I still feel that pain. Now I see why the prayers had me support either decision.

Shortly after she decided to stay, we thought we should get married. The decision to get married was because she would not be able to keep knowledge of the relationship from her parents very much longer, and partly because she had to let her parents know she was not going to Russia.

Second Near-Death Experience

I experienced a major internal conflict. I talked with people I respected, and I prayed. I was not attending a church regularly, but I did have my faith. During the summer, before leaving for college, I worked at a gas station. Standard Stations of California owned the gas station. I was able to transfer to a gas station near the school after I left for college. After relocating to the new gas station, I worked the night shift from 11 pm to 7 am. It was a Standard Stations policy to not keep more than twenty dollars of cash after 10 pm. One night a motorcycle gang of several riders drove into the station. When I walked out to meet them, one of them pulled a knife and demanded money. I told them about the policy regarding limited cash. They did not believe me. I thought they were going to kill me. I silently prayed as quickly as I could. I only asked what I should do.

I remember seeing the image of my grandmother in my mind. I thought this was very strange at first, but then I remembered something she told me. When I was five years old, and older boys at the park took my bicycle, my father told me to go back to the park and get it the bicycle.

I did not know what to do; they were older and stronger than me. My family was visiting my grandparents at the time. My grandmother talked to me in private. She said, remember one thing, "Nobody has balls of steel. If there are three of them, kick the middle one as hard as you can, and the other two will run." When I went back to get the bicycle, the plan worked as she said it would.

I immediately knew what the image of my grandmother meant. I kicked the one with the knife so hard it lifted him off the ground. He lay on the ground, crying, and the others left. I do not recommend this method of solving challenges to anyone, but I still believe it was the correct solution for that situation.

Deciding to Marry

I explained the entire situation about getting married to my parents. They were supportive. I needed their permission because in 1969, I was only nineteen years old, and the law required the male to be twenty-one years old to marry without parental consent. We married in January of 1970.

My parents made the arrangements for the wedding. We married at a judge's office. Then we went to my friend Casey's wedding and wedding/reception and finally had our reception at my parent's house.

Her parents did not know about the wedding. She told them the next day. Her father called my father and asked him if it was true. My father said yes, then her father hung up the phone.

Reception at My Parent's House

We lived in an apartment. I took classes during the day and practiced with the football team every afternoon and evening. She got a job, but she did not go to school. I felt more guilt. She was very supportive, but I never felt right about her not finishing college.

I still was not attending church. I maintained my faith, but I did not try to find a church to attend. Later I did regret not worshiping weekly.

Of course, the relationship with her parents had complications. They let us know we would be responsible for her student loans. I was okay with that.

After some time, the relationship with her family did improve. I never felt accepted by her parents, but I did feel close to her two sisters and her brother.

Being married, playing football, and attending college was a challenge, but we both enjoyed those years. My major was political science with a minor in economics. The football scholarship paid all my college expenses and the apartment rent. I worked part-time, and the football coach was able to get my wife an excellent full-time job with a technology company. Technology work was unusual back in 1969. We did well during those years. She always supported my sports.

At that time, I did pray regularly. I always felt the spirit. We did not face any significant challenges, so my main goal was to finish college and advance to the next step in my life.

I thanked God so many times for helping me have an open mind about moving from Paradise during my last day there. I could see how that move made so many things possible. During those college days, I developed many relationships that had positive effects on later years in my life. It became clear to me that praying for answers to something would frequently result in a clear understanding of the consequences that may result from specific choices. When I was very young, I thought God would solve problems. During my college years, I realized I was responsible for addressing my challenges, but a close relationship with Jesus would allow me to best review the options.

Important Lesson Learned

I always knew which options were appropriate, but when I was younger, I did not identify specific scriptures that stated the reasons. It was especially true when the deception was part of an answer. I knew to lie was wrong, but until I studied the New Testament, I did not understand many of the consequences of making the wrong decision. Sometimes I believed deception was acceptable if it did not hurt anyone. Of course, I learned this lesson when I experienced lies that seemed innocent but caused significant challenges much later.

I learned that to be honest; all the time would be much better for me overall. If I had challenges finishing college papers, it was easy to blame a football trip, but I had time during those trips to work on school projects. My coaches were very considerate when it came to allowing time for schoolwork. Professors were open to working with me based on the actual situation without an exaggerated story. These experiences helped me later in my life. It was another example of how honoring God's teaching made life better for me.

Vietnam War Causes Challenges

During the time I went to college, the American Government created a draft system requiring all males eighteen years old to register. The Draft was created to support the Vietnam War.

As I mentioned, I received a low number. That meant that I would be drafted to attend the military. I was depressed about this because I worked so hard to prepare myself to earn my way through college with a football scholarship, and it could be lost. There was an education deferment, but because of the class load, I had to allow time for football and work, I did not qualify.

I felt the same as I did during my last day at Paradise except, I had that experience to help me analyze the situation. Unlike that last day in Paradise, I prayed for guidance. I knew I did not wish to do anything illegal, such as going to Canada, as some of my friends did.

Unexpected Answer to Prayer

Unlike previous times, my prayers did not provide me with clarity regarding the consequences of each option. I knew the guidance would come from God, but I did not feel clarity.

The answer came two days later when two Marines gave a presentation to the football team before that day's practice. They presented a program where I could take an exam and provide consent to a background check. If I passed the exam and background check, I would have an oral interview. After giving the oral interview, I would have the option to attend the United States Marine Corps Officer Candidate School for two summers (six weeks each summer) in Quantico, Virginia.

If I completed the Officer Candidate School training and earned an undergraduate degree, I would become an officer in the Marine Corps.

Joining the Marine Corps was a significant decision. My father was in the Army during World War II and the Korean War, so he did not favor Marines. The American public was against the war by this time.

I was in another situation like Paradise; I did not want to go into the Marine Corps. This time I had the benefit of learning from the Paradise move. I knew I had to consider long-term consequences.

After praying, my first action was to check the other branches to see if they had similar programs. Then I checked the Peace Corps and other options. The Army and Air Force had officer programs, but those programs required strict attendance during the school year. I would not be able to play football and would lose my scholarship. Joining the Peace Corps would also mean losing the football scholarship.

I talked with my father about the situation. He said he wished I would join any other branch. Because the Marine Corps was the only service that allowed me to complete my undergraduate degree before becoming active, he supported the decision.

I was surprised my wife was supportive after we talked about it. She was not aware of the prayers, but she did understand the seriousness of my situation. She is the one who mentioned I would be going to war either way, at least this way; I had a chance to complete my undergraduate degree first.

Unfortunately, my wife's family did not share her view. They were firmly against the Vietnam War and were not supportive of the military. They could not understand how my wife was able to support this decision.

I passed the exam, the background check, and the oral interview. I was on a flight to Quantico, Virginia, two months after the Marine Corps presentation in the football locker room.

My father briefed me about what to expect during the Officer Candidate School. His advice was beneficial. He explained to me what the Marine Corps wanted to accomplish during the training. He let me know how to set my priorities. It helped to expect some of the experiences and understand what was important.

Commitment to the Marine Corps

While in Quantico, I made a lot of close friends and learned about other parts of the country. My first summer of Officer Candidate School was in 1969. The racial tensions were still very high, especially in Virginia.

I had another chance to see things the way they were, not the way I thought they were. Since I was from California, I had seen some racial prejudice, but not nearly as extreme as I saw in Virginia. I prayed a lot during that summer. There were so many things I did not understand.

There was a tremendous amount of stress. During my early years, I ignored racist people, but that was not possible during the training. I did not understand this. Some people would not drink from the water fountain because some of the group were black.

At first, I did my best to ignore the racist candidates, but there were so many of them. As I prayed and worked my way through the program, I learned I should not judge other people by one measurement. I needed to try to know a person and learn their history. It was essential to communicate with everyone and try to understand everyone's circumstances.

I had an advantage during the training because I was in good physical shape due to football training. However, academics and discipline training were extremely demanding. We would get up at 5 am and be busy until 10 or 11 pm. We did have time to rest on Sunday. It was strenuous, but the advice my father gave me helped.

Many of the candidates quit during the training ("DOR" an abbreviation for Drop on request). We lost over one-third of the class by the end of the first summer. It was sad to see new friends leave.

Finishing College

My time in college went very well. I loved learning as much as I could about political science. I graduated in 1972, Richard Nixon was the President of the United States. Of course, he was a major topic during many of the classes.

I remember thinking about Jesus and politics. My views of the world changed as I experienced life, but at that time, I was studying other people's lives. I remember how awful the killing of Martin Luther King and Robert Kennedy was. Robert Kennedy was the first person I actively supported for any political office. I believed in him. It was devesting the night he was shot. I was a senior in high school and did not understand how God could allow that to happen. I did not try to see any other views; I just thought it was wrong.

Much later, I realized many things happen for a reason. It is not my place to judge whether the reason justifies the original pain.

Many political figures would mention God when things were not going well. I always wondered why they did not talk about God when times were good.

I did work hard studying for my classes. It was difficult going to school, playing football, along with working a part-time job. I did not sleep at night because I worked from 10 pm to 6 am five days a week. It is incredible what you can do when you face challenges. I learned about analyzing situations, organizing my time, documenting research, and questioning thoughts from respected authorities.

I had several professors who taught me how to analyze situations and make judgments based on actual evidence. This ability was a tremendous asset later when I pursued Christianity directly.

Later in life, I learned that when I questioned the Bible, sometimes I was wrong. I worked to verify points that seem questionable to me. It helped me to see based on other evidence that my understanding of the scripture may not have been correct. However, in all cases applying the scripture made my life better.

My second summer in Officer Candidate School (1971) was beautiful because many of the candidates from the first summer were there. Since we already served one six-week session, the day to day schedule was not a surprise.

The pace was a little faster, and the academics were more detailed. Many members of our class dropped out during the second half of the session.

I can still remember praying some nights, asking God if I was doing the right thing. It was hard to address the fact I was training to kill people. Of course, the other side of that argument was that the war was for a better good. At that time, the public turned on the Vietnam War. The press was still neutral in their reporting of the war, but that was soon to change.

I felt strongly that I committed to serve, and I was going to satisfy that commitment. By the end of the six weeks, I was comfortable with my commitment to serve.

I would be a Marine Corps Officer upon college graduation, I felt good about my life. I did study more and felt like I had a future. My lifetime goal was to be in Congress but becoming an officer in the Marine Corps was secure and felt good at that moment.

I developed strong feelings about the direction of America. When I think back on those days, I am not sure what the inspiration was for the thoughts. I had a vision of technology changing the way America operated. It was clear to me that technology would replace many jobs. I did think the new opportunities would help young people. My understanding of the culture in America in 1971 was that it was still necessary to build things in America. Foreign automobiles were becoming popular partly because of the initial lower prices.

By the time I graduated, America was beginning to use significant labor from overseas. The overseas jobs were a subject I thought about often. At first, it was like the experience of leaving Paradise. I thought it was all negative. I was one of the people that did not believe all advances were good.

My Final Paper

After I returned from Officer Candidate School, I talked with two of my professors about overseas jobs. They both saw them as unfavorable for America. I was completing my last primary political science class. Since my minor was in economics, I read plenty of information that supported overseas jobs to improve the economy.

Just like when I left Paradise, I thought about the overseas jobs and have dreams about the potential. After some time, I did not pray but had strong feelings about God and what was right. From that process, I began to write the draft for my final paper. After I reviewed my deep feelings, I was able to understand how I felt. I saw overseas jobs as an opportunity. I realized many of the people in third world countries were working very long days, seven days a week in some cases, and for low wages.

My thoughts were that there were many jobs that Americans did not wish to work, and the technology was an opportunity for Americans to have better jobs.

The third world country wages were the first time I can remember beginning to consider people from other countries and think about what was right for them. When drafting the college paper, I made several points. 1) Technology is going to come, and we must adjust to it. 2) New, better jobs will result. 3) We can help people in third world countries.

I spent my initial time researching the paper. At that time, there were no computers, not even word processing. I had to go to the library and read significant sections from many books. After reading as much as I could, I saw we had an opportunity.

The idea I developed was to create laws in America that would apply American labor laws to overseas jobs. If a company were American based and hired employees in other countries, the federal labor laws would apply to the foreign workers.

I felt terrific about the idea. The concept was for America to raise the standard of living in other countries. I thought this approach would help the people of third world countries, and America would continue to create better, higher-paying jobs in America.

I worked hard on the paper. Since there were no copy machines, word processors, or printers, my wife typed the paper for me. Unfortunately, there was no copy of my paper; so, I cannot review it.

Unfortunately, America followed an approach that was the opposite of my paper. Instead of raising the standard of living in third world countries, we reduced the standard of living in America. By the '80s, corporations sent thousands of jobs to third world countries for low wages and no benefits and put Americans out of work.

Although America did not move the direction I presented, the events of the time changed my view of the world, and I changed my priorities when thinking about people. During prior years, my thoughts about people were directed at Americans and did not consider the challenges of people in other countries.

Part of the reason for this change in thinking was learning in Sunday School at church about the distinction Jesus made between the government of Rome and the Christian movement. I realized the government of Rome was separate from following Jesus.

Governments have the purpose of supporting the needs of the people they serve at the time and protecting the people from each other, from natural disasters and foreign enemies. The government provides order and works to improve life for all its citizens. The government can be evil when its leaders promote their interests ahead of the benefits of the people they serve.

The Christian movement taught individual people how to live. Of course, this movement has no borders. The teachings of Jesus apply to everyone equally. Governments created laws that are also in the Bible, such as lying, stealing, murder, etc. However, the rules in the Bible do not recognize borders.

By the time I completed college, I understood the distinction between government and Christianity. However, at that time I still wanted to become part of the government as an elected member of congress.

My Grandfather Dies

Near the end of my third year of college in 1971, my maternal grandfather died. He was very special to me. When I was a child, I wanted to be like him. He was a supervisor in Northern California. My impression of him was that he always understood what was necessary. He was a Christian and lived life honestly.

When my mother was in junior high school, my grandfather was deceived by a man who stole everything my grandfather had. My grandfather's family had to live in a tent and did not have enough food for over a year.

He never lost faith. He worked with an attorney from Los Angeles to challenge the situation. Eventually, he won a lawsuit that restored his financial status.

I learned a great lesson from my grandfather's experience. Regardless of how bad his situation became, he kept his family together, did not lose faith in God, and eventually overcame all his challenges. He was a strong example to all those around him. I wanted to be like him.

Many years later, I thought about how things my parents and grandparents did had a strong positive impact on my life. In every case, they showed a commitment to continuing to work toward solving challenges aided by a faith that God would guide them to understand the consequences of making the wrong decisions.

While I was still in college, I learned about a similar situation regarding my other grandfather. He was a coal miner in Pennsylvania during the depression in the 1930s. The challenge of supporting a family during those times was significant. The coal companies were charging for housing, groceries, and other incidentals. My grandfather had three children. It was challenging for him to provide for his family.

In that family, my grandmother was the head of the family. She made all decisions and kept everyone in line. I remember she controlled the entire family. However, this one time, my grandfather made a decision that was against my grandmother's choice.

He decided to quit his job and drive the family to California. He decided they would sell everything they could and leave. He would try to get a job as quickly as he could. My grandmother was against this plan. She thought it made no sense to quit his work when there were no other jobs available. She protested, but my grandfather said the correct decision was to quit his job and move west.

The family with three children, the oldest was my father (six years old), had a total of $360 when they left for California.

They used as little of their money as possible during the trip. Luckily, my grandparents did not experience any automobile challenges even though their car was old. They made it to Arizona. During the trip, my grandfather had a list of all his relatives and friends who lived in the West. The first two he visited had no leads for work. Then they arrived in Arizona where he talked with a friend who worked at the Hoover Dam in Arizona. His friend was able to get him a job that would last for almost two years (until that portion of the Dam project was complete). He had to interview for a job as a carpenter. He had no carpenter skills at that time. He did his best during the interview and convinced the company he had good work references, was a quick learner, and he needed the work.

He received an answer to his prayer. He was able to get the job. He quickly developed excellent skills as a carpenter. The work was so much healthier than working in the coal mines. He earned enough money for his family to live appropriately, and they were able to save enough money to continue their trip to California.

After his work with the Hoover Dam was complete, he immediately moved the entire family to Northern California where the state was building the Shasta Dam. He was hired immediately as a carpenter.

The family made a permanent home in Northern California. The family still lives there to this day.

My grandfather's decision to quit his job and move West was the most important decision he would make. My grandfather did not tell me directly that God told him to make that decision. I believe God gave him guidance regarding the resolution, and my grandfather thought he needed to go against the feelings of everyone else. I believe this because I experienced the same situation later in my life, although it was not as drastic as my grandfather's decision. I talk about that situation in another chapter in this book.

Thirty years after the move, it was clear my grandfather's family benefited from a much stronger financial position than all their relatives who stayed in the East. The one time he made a strong stand had a more significant impact on his family and the descendants of his family than any other decision in his life.

At the time I first heard about this decision, I did not understand the importance. When I had a family of my own, I realized he had solid faith in Jesus to make that decision without any other support.

The decisions we make can affect people for generations. It is critical to do what is right, not what seems to be most rewarding at the time. God has given us the power of free moral will, but he also offers guidance if we ask for it.

I was so blessed to have come from a family with a strong faith in God. In many cases, I made the right decisions because my family members faced more significant challenges and chose the right choices instead of the most rewarding options.

Although I mentioned the two big decisions from both my grandfathers, my father made excellent choices his entire life. He always helped everyone else. He was a terrific example for me.

Many times, I thought about decisions my mother and father made that helped me analyze my situation. My mother and father thought about how their actions would affect others before making a critical decision.

Football in College

Football in college worked very well for me. Not only did my scholarship pay for my education, I learned how to apply myself and compete against people with better natural ability. I believe my faith helped me to compete at all levels and not allow significant challenges to distract me from doing my best.

The reason I did not wish to leave Paradise was because I did not think I could begin at a new school halfway through my junior year in high school. I did not realize I could compete well enough to earn a football scholarship. As it turned out, I became the best athlete in the Southern California school and had my choice of several major universities to play football.

Earlier in this book, I mentioned the message, "to work hard for the benefit of the team, not to focus on what would benefit me." That message continued to drive my effort in college. The other players responded positively to me immediately. I received plenty of credit without trying for it. Helping the team to achieve success was more gratifying, and the honesty of my play was noticeable.

I tried not to use football as an excuse to miss work in my classes. It was clear the classwork was the main reason I was at the college; football was the way I paid the tuition. The coach did not appreciate my attitude all the time, but I worked hard enough not to disappoint the coach. There were occasions when I had to miss practice because of a course requirement, such as attending a City Council meeting. At first, the coach tried to pressure me not to participate in the course event. After the second time, he realized my study was a higher priority than football practice. In the end, he respected me for always being honest with them.

Every time I was honest when addressing a challenge, the result was positive in the long run. I was honest with the coaches about my priorities. Although, I did have to think before I communicated my preference to the coaches. I knew it could eventually cause me to lose my scholarship. After much thought and some prayer, I did tell the coaches my priority was schoolwork. The coaches said not to worry, that they would talk with my professors and make sure the professors excused me. I told the coaches I did not wish to be excused from class events unless we had an actual game. It was challenging, but after a couple of weeks, the stress left. I felt right about being honest with the coaches, the professors, my fellow students, and my fellow teammates. I could focus on the tasks that were important to me and not feel guilty about not being able to give 100% to everything.

Major Disappointment

I had one significant disappointment halfway through my senior year in college. I had an opportunity to go to Graduate School at Harvard University. I was so excited, and my wife was also thrilled. I would have a better chance of being accepted in her family if I went to Harvard Graduate School.

However, Harvard University made a public stand against the Vietnam War. Part of their commitment was they would not allow the military to recruit personnel on the Harvard campus. Then the Department of the Navy said no Navy or Marine Corps personnel on active duty could attend Harvard University. Losing the opportunity to study at Harvard was another situation where I was very depressed and thought my lifelong goal was in jeopardy.

My next step was to try to go to law school. Law school was also a part of my long-term dream. However, the commitment I made to the Marine Corps did not allow me to delay going on active duty beyond my graduation date from undergraduate school.

Initially, I did not learn from the vision during the last day I was in Paradise. I did not think that this situation was part of a plan for me. Other opportunities would present themselves that may be more supportive of my life objective.

Disappointment Turned to Opportunity

As it turned out, after I reported for active duty, in June of 1972, I discovered that the University of Southern California (USC) supported the Marine Corps. USC had a campus in Okinawa, Japan that helped active-duty American military personnel stationed in Vietnam. I was able to enroll in the Graduate School of Business and earn a master's degree in Public Administration. I was able to take advantage of business opportunities because USC had a strong presence in Southern California. I will discuss those opportunities later in the book.

The fact that football season was over on January 1, 1972, meant I had the entire semester to focus entirely on schoolwork and my job, no football practice or traveling. It was an opportunity to look at the Southern California community and analyze what we should do to help advance to a level where life is better than it was for the previous generation.

At the end of the semester, my conclusion was that the next generation would be the first generation that will not live in better conditions than the previous generation.

Part of the cause may be that the future generation did not have to sacrifice as much, and their parents were in a better position to support them than previous generations.

My conclusion was that the middle-class Americans began to lose earning power when compared to previous generations after compensation is adjusted based on the value of the dollar of each generation.

By the time I graduated, I realized that America did the opposite of my vision. Instead of America using labor from other countries to raise the standard of living in third world countries, corporations began exploiting third world countries at the expense of the American working class.

When I was very young, it was essential to buy products made in America. People considered the lives of other Americans. By the time I graduated, Americans wanted products at the lowest price. The country that built the product did not matter.

I was thrilled to reach graduation day, but I was also sad about the direction of America. I thought about the vision I had regarding football when I left Paradise. The concept was to work hard to help the team. I began to see how this concept affected how we work in America and all over the world. If everyone is working to make life better for all, the standard of living for the individual would rise. I learned from playing high school football in Southern California and college that playing as hard as I could to help the team was better for me as well as everyone else. One key factor was, do not directly seek credit for anything. It was critical not to work hard for personal gain alone. There is no problem with accepting personal gain when it comes as part of the improvement for everyone else.

Even in the early 1970s, most elected officials did not work hard for the good of the country, and they sought personal praise or financial support.

Although clear back in 1972, I did understand the disappointing direction America was going, I still had my lifetime goal of becoming a member of Congress. I believed I could make a difference from inside Congress. However, that objective would have to wait because, on graduation day, I was sworn in as an officer in the Marine Corps and left the next day to report to the Marine Corps Basic School in Quantico, Virginia.

CHAPTER 5

MARINE CORPS

The Drive to Quantico

I drove to the Marine Recruit Depot in San Diego as soon as I completed my graduation in June of 1972. General Mclaughlin was the Commanding General. He commissioned me as a Second Lieutenant. It was strange because the General commissioned three officers during the ceremony, but I was the only one who did not have a uniform. I wore a suit. I wore the suit because I graduated that day; I was not qualified to purchase uniforms before graduation. I had to wait until I arrived in Quantico to wear a uniform.

My Commission Ceremony

The day after my graduation, my wife and I left in our car for the cross-country trip to Quantico, Virginia. The trip took a week. It was nice to see other parts of the country. I knew I was beginning a new section of my life. I was not sure what to expect.

I did have conflicting thoughts about being in the Marine Corps. As a committed Christian, was it wrong to be in the Marine Corps? At that time in my life, some things seemed acceptable but became challenges later. The Vietnam War was becoming unpopular. I had friends from high school who were killed in Vietnam.

Although I was depressed when receiving news, people I knew died in the war, I felt America needed people who were committed to defending freedom. I thought that was what I was doing. At that time, I thought my obligation was to follow orders and help provide a defense for our country. I felt it was the government's responsibility to decide if a war was just or not. I thought the government worked in the best interest of the people. Years later, I realized this belief was the way it should be, but it is evident that the public interest is not the priority of the government.

After starting the Basic School, I began to feel serving in the Marine Corps did support my Christian beliefs.

As one might expect, the Basic School was extremely efficient. We learned all aspects of being an officer.

There were formal classes about six hours a day with a break for lunch and a few minutes between every session. The classroom training was extremely organized. The subjects covered included everything from the chain of command to parades. I experienced actual tactics, battle training, and command exercises in training areas on the Quantico base.

There was also physical training every day, such as exercises, runs, and long hikes with full packs. We had inspections on a scheduled and surprise basis. The entire program felt comprehensive, and the overall experience was much more professional than the Officer Candidate School. The objective of the Officer Candidate School was to qualify potential officers. The Basic School aimed to prepare new officers. It was much more comprehensive and demanding than college.

I did experience an environment that was consistent with my Christian beliefs. That seems strange when learning how to kill people is a significant part of the training. The aspect of life in the Marine Corps that seemed consistent with Christian teaching was the honesty, accepting responsibility for one's actions, and working together to help everyone.

The third point, working together to help everyone, was especially important. I did not understand how important this concept was until more than ten years later. It was the same concept I learned when I began playing football in Southern California. I did understand that the only goal was making the success of the team. The idea of supporting the team allowed me to be successful in Southern California. But I did not see the big picture. This concept applies to everything. I should have already understood this concept before entering the Marine Corps, but I had to experience it several times. I still had difficulty seeing the connection of working to help other people while never personally taking credit for achievement helped to improve life for everyone.

Later in this book, I will discuss many other examples of times when helping others helped me be successful.

It was when I studied the Sermon on the Mount that I saw so many times in my life that I benefited from the teaching of Jesus. In some cases, I had dreams. In other cases, I simply had a very strong feeling inside to do what I knew was right, not what would benefit me.

During the six months in the Basic School I felt the concept of working for the good of everyone and not taking credit for accomplishments. I continued to be comfortable with the outcome.

I learned the concept of leadership much more directly than when I played college football. When working on specific challenges with a team of other members of the class, I saw firsthand how frequently the real leaders are not the designated leaders. There were times when members of a team would provide insight that made their team members look better, yet they did not take credit for the outcome.

There were many instructors who helped me develop skills I would use the rest of my life. One of those instructors became nationally known fifteen years later. His name was Captain Oliver North. He was my patrolling instructor.

Oliver North gave 100% effort to the task he was performing. As an instructor, he took his task so seriously he would create environments that were like combat even though we were in a classroom.

One example is when he was teaching a specific patrolling technique. He arrived at class in full combat dress with his face camouflaged and he had an M16 rifle. The entire lesson was a simulation of an actual patrol and was conducted in a classroom, not out in the field. About two-thirds of the way through the session, Oliver North yelled several commands and fired his M16 rifle multiple times. He had blanks in his gun, but it shocked everyone in the class. I will never forget that moment. We felt the terror of the challenges many of us faced months later. I only knew Oliver North for those few months, but he left an impression with me. Everything I saw him do was for the benefit of those around him.

Fifteen years later, when Oliver North was a Lieutenant Colonel in the Marine Corps, he was assigned to the NSA when Ronald Regan was President. He testified at congressional hearings for the Iran-Contra hearings.

Although he had gone through a lot during those fifteen years since I was a student of his, I could still see his commitment to honesty and supporting all those around him. Based on stories from the press, Oliver North had mental challenges and other issues. When he testified, I saw the same Oliver North that gave 100% to every class he taught.

I had several instructors who taught me the importance of focus and supporting all those around me.

My original plan when joining the Marine Corps was to serve in the Infantry. I had friends who went into the Marine Corps right after high school, and they all went to the Infantry. The rest of the Marine Corps supports the Infantry.

However, not everything in Basic School was positive. Three independent incidents happened during the last three months that were almost more than I could bear. The entire Marine Corps structure taught me so much, and later, I did see the similarities to what I learned from Christian teachings. I thought not only did I want to be in the Infantry, but it was where I thought God wanted me to be. I did not see myself as a killer but as a protector. Many times, in the Bible, biblical leaders fought in wars and attacked the enemy. I had reconciled that concept. Three incidents shattered my desire to serve in the Infantry.

Challenges with Pregnancy

My wife and I learned she was pregnant during the first two months of the Basic School. We were both so happy; this was such a blessing. My wife became close friends with several of the other wives.

My wife was supportive of my effort at the Basic School. Even though she was against the Vietnam War at that time, she supported me completely. She attended all wives' functions, and she adjusted to the role of an officer's wife with no resistance.

After a few weeks, she began to have challenges with the pregnancy. She suffered pain, and the doctor was concerned. The situation became more severe but seemed manageable.

A ceremony called "Mad Moment" was scheduled for my class. The Mad Moment was an evening event where large artillery equipment was beside the bleacher seats. Tanks drove into the area. Marine Corps jets were flying in the area.

During the Mad Moment Ceremony, the artillery would fire live rounds of ammunition. The tanks would fire at targets to the right and left of the bleacher seats. Then jets would fly toward the group and drop ordinance on targets within eyesight of the bleachers.

The Mad Moment is a spectacular event. The noise was deafening, the fire was visible, and you could feel an energetic vibration.

The challenge was that the doctor told my wife she should not be around loud noises or vibrations during her pregnancy because of her condition.

During a morning formation, the commanding officer told everyone in our class that the Mad Moment Ceremony was mandatory for all wives to attend. The Marine Corps wanted the wives to understand how dramatic the training was.

That night when I told my wife about the ceremony, she told me what the doctor said about avoiding loud noises and vibrations. I told her I would talk with the Company Commander the next morning.

When I met with my Company Commander and told him about the doctor's instruction, he told me she had to attend the ceremony. He said he would talk with the doctor and he would make sure there was enough emergency medical support available.

I talked with my wife about the conversation with the Company Commander. She was not happy about it. I made a call to one of the instructors I respected. He told me the Marine Corps could order my wife to attend the ceremony. If she refused, I could be court-martialed and discharged from the Marine Corps.

That law was abolished in the late 1970s, but at that time the Marine Corps could tell an officer's wife what to do. Officer's wives were not allowed to work unless they had written permission from the Marine Corps. Working as a nurse was one of the few jobs the Marine Corps would enable officers to wives to do. Officer's wives were expected to do significant amounts of charity work. When Marine Corps Officers were assigned "unaccompanied tours," generally for thirteen months to places like Vietnam or Japan, the wives were not allowed to accompany their husbands.

When I talked with my wife about what the instructor said, I did my best to give her all the consequences of not attending. She felt the doctor said it was a precaution, and she was feeling better. She did not wish to cause me legal challenges and decided to participate in the ceremony.

As soon as the artillery began to fire, she felt significant amounts of pain. The medical staff took both of us to the hospital. She miscarried. I spent the night with her at the hospital.

The Company Commander was informed about the incident. He came to the hospital early the next morning. I approached him and let him know my wife had a miscarriage. He had no emotion. He said she probably would have lost the baby eventually anyway. Then he told me I had to leave the hospital and put on my dress uniform because our company was in a parade that morning.

I could not believe he asked me to do that. I made sure my wife was recovering without a challenge. Then I went home and changed for the parade.

I had a tough time accepting that situation. I wanted out of the Marine Corps. I talked with my wife, and she told me she still supported me in the Marine Corps and would manage to recover from the situation after some time. She said she had no problem with me staying in the Marine Corps.

Of course, I lost respect for my Company Commander, but I did my best to continue in the Basic School.

My Birth Father Dies

The second incident that changed my mind about joining the Infantry started with a message I received from the Red Cross. The note said my birth father killed himself nine months earlier, November 1971, but it took them this long to reach me.

I felt devastated. I knew I was wrong for not staying in touch with my birth father, especially after he made efforts to contact me. I had a solid feeling I should visit his family and learn much more about him. By this time, I knew there was a lot more to his story than my grandmother told me.

Then I contacted his brother's wife. She let me know he shot himself near their home in Fort Worth, Texas. When she told me the actual date, I was shocked. I played a football game in Arlington,

Texas, the night he shot himself. I felt so much guilt. After learning the date, I thought I had to see his family and pay my respects.

The next day I had a meeting with my Company Commander. I explained the entire situation to him. I told him I needed some time off to visit my birth father's family. I made it clear I would be gone a week at the most, and I would make up any work I missed.

He told me that because it had been nine months since my birth father shot himself, it was not urgent. He said I would have some leave time at the end of the Basic School in three months and I could visit the family then.

I could not believe what he told me. I talked to my wife. Then I spoke with the Commanding Officer of the Basic School. I understood the Company Commander had the authority to authorize leave, and he had the power to deny a leave request as well. He explained to me there was no review. I would not be able to take leave until the end of the Basic School.

I talked with my wife, and we decided we did not like the situation, but it was probably better that we go after the Basic School so there would not be as much pressure when we stayed with my birth father's family.

I was not happy with the situation, but I did feel we made the correct decision.

We went to Texas after I finished Basic School, and we met with my birth father's family. After meeting with his family, I felt so guilty for not contacting them many years earlier. I should have met with him and asked about what my grandparents told me about him.

The information my grandparents gave me about him was not even close to what his family shared with me.

His family told me about an automobile accident; my birth father was in during his senior year in high school. He was the only survivor. He recovered from the medical damage but had mental challenges. He tried to enlist in the Army, but they rejected him for psychological reasons. Then he enlisted in the Marine Corps, and they accepted him.

During World War II he was stationed in the South Pacific. The enemy shot him during a battle that destroyed most of his battalion.

There were no leaders that survived. He was severely wounded and had to fend for himself for over two days. After being rescued, he recovered from the injuries, but his mental challenges became much worse. His family told me he became an alcoholic shortly after he returned from the war. They said it was the only way he could live.

I could not believe my grandparents did not know about his sacrifices.

I immediately felt pain for not addressing the situation when my grandparents first told me the negative information. Maybe I was too young to know better at that time, but by the time I was in high school, I had met with him several times. I should have asked him about his challenges. If I had followed Christian beliefs, I would have known to address that situation as early as possible. Just a year ago when I taught the Bible Study lesson on the Sermon on the Mount, that exact situation was addressed. I made that same error multiple times in my life.

Night Compass March

The third incident during the Basic School Class that changed my mind about joining the Infantry happened during an event called the "Night Compass March." This event was conducted late at night. The instructor gave me a map with specific checkmarks. When I arrived at each location, there was a container with a sheet of paper inside the container. The piece of paper had a code on it. There were several checkpoints. Before returning to the starting point, I was required to document the code for each checkpoint.

I did well during the first three checkpoints. I quickly found the containers and wrote the codes on my form. On my way to the fourth checkpoint, I felt a severe pain near my stomach.

I continued to walk toward the next checkpoint, but the pain became more severe. I immediately changed course toward the one road in that area. It was about eleven at night, and I was in the middle of the woods on the base by myself.

I was able to walk to the road. I fell on the ground, and the pain was almost unbearable. I was on the ground for a little while and thought I was going to die.

A jeep appeared on the road. I was able to wave my arm, and the vehicle stopped and took me to the hospital.

By the time I arrived at the hospital, the training staff already briefed the hospital personnel about my situation. Within fifteen minutes, the doctor determined my appendix burst.

The nurses took me to a surgery room, and the procedure to remove my appendix was performed.

Before going into surgery, the doctor explained to me that the hospital staff had updated everyone at the Night Compass March about my situation. I asked the doctor if the hospital staff had notified my wife. He said not yet, but his team was updating my Company Commander, and the Company Commander would talk with my wife.

After the way my Company Commander handled the previous two incidents, I did not want my Company Commander to talk with my wife. I told the doctor the Company Commander does not have enough empathy to calmly and thoughtfully communicate the right message to my wife. The doctor said not to worry and that he would make sure someone else talked with my wife.

The surgery was successful. When I was in the recovery room, my wife came to see how I was doing. She was agitated. She said the Company Commander went to our house after midnight. He told her I collapsed along the road, and he did not know at that time if the surgery would be successful. She went through significant stress again, and again, it was unnecessary.

After talking with her, I knew the Infantry was not for me. I was in the hospital for several days recovering. I reported back to my company after seven days.

Alternatives to the Infantry

After experiencing all three incidents, I knew I did not wish to be in the infantry. Within two weeks, all Basic School attendees in this class would have to submit three choices for the MOS to be assigned. MOS is a Military Occupational Specialty and includes Infantry, Artillery, Supply, Technology, Military Police, and many others.

I reviewed the details for all the choices available to me. After reviewing all the available options, I realized the Marine Corps had two sections. The first section was ground that included Infantry, Artillery, Supply, etc. The other part of the Marine Corps was the Air Wing. They were two completely different organizations that reported to the Commandant of the Marine Corps.

I immediately concluded I wanted to be in the Air Wing. The MOS Staff told me the only option that would work for me was to go to flight school and become a Marine Corps aviator.

I was not qualified for that choice. I had never flown a plane, I had taken no aerodynamics courses, and I did not participate in any flight training programs. My lack of flight experience was very depressing.

I prayed for help. I knew the Air Wing was where I needed to be. It is strange because I never wished to be a pilot. I always wanted to be a lawyer. Now being a Marine Corps Aviator was extremely important to me.

In my prayers, I did not ask God to make me a pilot. I asked for help finding all the options to become a pilot. I was willing to compete to become an aviator even if everyone else had the advantage of flight experience, aerodynamics education, and flight simulation training.

I prayed for three days asking for help to find a way to access the program. Then I met with one of my instructors, who was a Marine Corps aviator. He told me that even if the MOS Team did select me for Flight School, I would be competing with everyone else who had prepared for many years. He did not think it was possible for me to be successful. He said half of the students who begin Flight School fail before they earn their wings. However, he told me I still had six days to apply for the Flight School exam. If I passed the exam, there would be two more steps, including an interview with a group of officers and a flight physical. After going through all three steps successfully, then I could compete with other Basic School attendees for selection to Flight School.

God answered my prayers; I did find a way to apply to Flight School. However, the odds of successfully competing for an assignment to Flight School were not good. Then the odds of completing Flight School and earning my wings were almost zero.

I felt a lot of stress. I did not feel prepared to compete. The other students had much more experience.

I prayed for help with the decision. I had several dreams that night. When I awoke the next morning, I had strong feelings like the way I felt the last day in Paradise. I thought there was no way I could compete to play football in Southern California. It was when I had the vision that working for the team was my goal, not trying to make myself look good. Suddenly the situation with Flight School did not seem as impossible as the earlier situation with the football team. The same concept applied. I needed to approach the flight school class in a way like I approached the Southern California high school football team. I needed to be as helpful as I could even though my background was behind the others, and I needed to treat everyone in the class as friends, not competitors. When I thought about how unlikely it was for me to succeed on the football team after moving to Southern California, I realized that situations are not always what they seem.

I decided to take the first step and register for the Flight School examination. The test date was only two days later, so I had no time to prepare. I prayed for guidance regarding how to approach the exam. For an unknown reason, I felt confident about being able to pass.

I felt strange on the morning of the exam. I was not nervous about the exam, and I felt like I made an excellent decision to take the exam.

When I started answering the questions, I was confused about some of them. The format was multiple choice. One of the sections was related to physics. I was not sure what the right answers were for that section. I decided to go with my first feeling.

I was fortunate that there were questions based on mathematics. Although I was a political science major in college, mathematics was my favorite subject. Many of my electives were related to mathematics.

For the questions relating directly to flying, I went with my first feeling.

After completing the exam, I felt nervous. I knew there was nothing else I could do. I had to wait for the results. After a morning formation, my Commanding Officer let me know I passed the exam. I could tell he was not pleased, but I was happy. I still had the physical exam and the oral interview. If I made it through those two hurdles, I still had to compete in flight school to earn my wings. I had a long way to go, but that night I felt good.

The physical took a full day. It was much more comprehensive than I had ever experienced. Once I passed the physical exam, they scheduled for the oral interview.

The oral interview was the most challenging of the three steps. The night before the meeting, I prayed for guidance. This time I told God I knew I did not deserve guidence because I had not been attending church regularly for almost two years. I followed his guidance both now and in the future. The intense feeling about putting the team first and my interest last and making sure to be a team player who does not shy from significant challenges helped me. By the time I awoke the next morning, I felt ready for the interview.

There were several officers present. At first, the questions were about my history. I let them know about things I experienced that may apply such as projects in school, preparing for college football games, and being on the debate team. Supporting the team was the bases for each answer. I was careful to be honest with every answer. That was a good point because the interview was over two hours long, and several times, the interviewers asked the same question in a slightly different format. If my answers were not consistent, I would have failed the interview.

When they asked me technical questions, I only answered the ones I understood. Even with those, if I was not positive about the answer, I told them what I thought was the answer but that I would need to verify to know for sure. If I had no idea what the answer was, I said so. I was surprised I was able to address three-fourths of the questions correctly. There were some questions I could not answer.

At the end of the interview, the officers were non-committal. I knew I did my best. If I did not pass, it might mean I should not go to flight school.

The next morning, the Battalion Office summoned me. I was nervous. One of the officers from the interview was waiting for me. He was very professional. He told me I was a weak Flight School candidate based on my experience, my technology knowledge, and my lack of flight experience. However, the Marine Corps had a shortage of aviators, and most of the officers in the interview gave me a passing recommendation.

One day after graduating from the Basic School, I was on my way to Pensacola, Florida, to attend flight school.

I did see that the situation the last day in Paradise was like the situation preparing for the Flight School interview and later preparing for flight school itself. Working for the benefit of all those around me instead of trying to make myself look good was the critical factor in my success. In each case, although supporting the people around me was my goal, my personal life did benefit. I should have studied the Sermon on The Mount back when I was in high school. Following those instructions would have made my life less stressful. I would have benefited even more, along with all those around me.

On the Way to Flight School

It was amazing. Two weeks after being accepted as a student in Flight School, I was leaving Quantico, Virginia for Pensacola,

Florida. I did take some leave time. My wife decided she wanted to go back to college while I was in Flight School. We both thought it was a good idea since Flight School was so demanding.

My wife talked to her parents. She transferred from the University of California, Santa Barbara to the University of California, Los Angeles (UCLA). My wife's parents lived close enough to UCLA that she could live with them and commute to school.

I felt good about her going back to school for several reasons, but one primary reason was that I felt so guilty she left college instead of going to Russia. Going to UCLA would not come close to replacing everything she lost, but it was an effort to restore some of what she lost. She was so good to me. She put my education and the Marine Corps first ahead of her ambitions. I was always extremely grateful for her efforts to support my goals.

My wife's behavior was much more consistent with Christianity than my practice at that time, yet I was the Christian, and she was agnostic. I wish I had worked harder to share Christianity with her.

As I mentioned earlier in this book, we drove from Quantico to Fort Worth, Texas, to visit the family of my birth father. I was so glad we tried to visit them. I met two of my birth father's brothers and the children of his brothers. The wife of one of his brothers knew much more about what happened to my birth father in World War II and what was on his mind the day he killed himself. Based on everything I heard from his entire family, he was a quality person and supported everyone around him. He never recovered mentally, and they said it was true he was an alcoholic. His brother's wife told me that on the day he shot himself, he told her he was not in control of his life and could not move forward or backward. The police found his body inside his truck. The damage to cars parked on each side of his vehicle made it clear he had been moving forward then backward several times before he shot himself.

His family told me my grandmother (my birth father's mother) was a full-blooded Choctaw Indian from Louisiana. I was fascinated by the stories about my birth father.

When I told his family, I was playing a football game in Austin, Texas, the very night he shot himself, they told me not to blame myself for not contacting him. They were good people, but I knew I was wrong. I would never be able to correct that wrong. My birth father needed me, and I was not there for him.

Chet Mayo, My Birth Father

After visiting my birth father's family, we drove to Southern California. My wife completed the paperwork for her to transfer to UCLA, so we arrived at her parent's house. Her family was kind to me, but it was clear they were not happy with me.

When we had dinner the first night, my wife's brother was there with his wife. He started saying very negative things about the Marine Corps and the Vietnam War. He is a nice person, but he was firmly against the Vietnam War. I was shocked when my wife's mother told him he was not informed. She said the Marine Corps treated her daughter with respect. She said her daughter was able to live the life of an officer's wife which meant she worked with essential charities and worked to help her community and she did not wish to hear negative talk about the Marine Corps anymore.

Again, although her family was agnostic, they did share many Christian beliefs. They always cared about helping other people. I did not see that when I first met them because they also put other people down if the other people did not share their priorities. I had difficulty understanding what they believed. I wish I knew more about my own beliefs at that time and shared some of those beliefs with them.

I drove from California to Florida in two days to report to Flight School. When I arrived and reported for duty, I did not know anyone. I reported to the officer's quarters. My roommate was from the Naval Academy.

The Flight School was part of the Navy, but both Marine Corps and Naval officers attended Flight School. The flight instructors included both Navy and Marine Corps aviators as well.

Flight School – the Ultimate Challenge

I started flight school in April of 1973. I was on the main base in Pensacola during the first three weeks of ground school. The classes included aeronautical engineering and basic flight rules.

After the initial ground school courses were complete, we moved to Saufley Field to begin flight training. My class was the first class to attend the ground school courses on demand. At first, we would have one flight a day. Then we could spend the remainder of our time studying the ground school or taking the tests for ground school. There were lessons to read and some lectures to attend. Then we took tests. Each student moved at their own pace. When the weather was not appropriate to fly, we worked on ground school all-day.

We also spent time in link trainers (a cockpit in a room with the stick, instruments, and other controls). We could practice our flight procedures and learn the details of the instrument panel. The airplane we flew was called a T-34. It was a single engine aircraft with two seats front and back.

It was at this time I felt the most stress. I knew I was far behind the skill level of all the other students. It was hard to sleep at night. I was always worried the program would drop me.

I prayed every night. I wanted help to reduce stress. However, the pressure did not go away the entire eighteen months I was in flight school. I had to work with fear, but eventually, I did learn how to prepare for the flights.

During my first flight, the instructor did most of the flying. He showed me all the necessary procedures, and after twenty minutes, he had me take control. My instructor was a Marine Corp Captain, and he was also the Safety Officer. The Marine Corps instructors were stricter.

That first flight was more challenging than I expected. I had no other experience even close to the experience of that flight.

During the second flight, I had to do the take-off and landing by myself. The landing was terrifying. However, the most challenging part was using a map to navigate while I was trying to fly the airplane. Of course, there was no GPS back then. I did manage to fly the plane back to the runway and did a somewhat smooth landing.

After surviving the first two flights, I knew I was in for the greatest challenge of my life. Playing football in Southern California was not even close to the pressure of working my way through flight school without any flying experience.

My third flight went well. I had a smooth take-off, navigated to all the checkpoints without challenge, and found the correct runway. All my radio calls were right, and the instructor seemed pleased. He gave me above average grades for the flight.

I did very well with the ground school. It was much easier to study and answer questions on tests than to go to the flight line and perform as directed.

I became more stressed every day. I knew I would have to work very hard for the first couple of months to become as comfortable as the other students. I prayed for help often. I studied all the procedures so thoroughly that I did not have to think about what to do.

After the first three flights, I was very comfortable. When the instructor created an emergency by cutting power or turning off systems, I always knew what to do. The challenge was being smooth when executing the procedures.

During the fourth flight, we had to create stalls and recover from them. I did fine with the stalls, but when the instructor asked me to initiate a spin and recover from it, I pushed the nose of the airplane too far down, and the instructor took control of the aircraft. The instructor failed me on the flight.

Failing this flight was a significant blow to my chances of graduating and receiving Aviator Wings. Each flight student was allowed one failed grade. A second failed flight required to stand in front of a Student Pilot Disposition Board. Usually, if a student stood before the Student Pilot Disposition Board, it resulted in a transfer from flight school.

After the failed flight, I received two practice flights and an instructor change before flying the fifth scheduled flight. There were ten scheduled flights before the first solo flight.

The stress was so intense I was unable to sleep at night. After I prayed, I remember feeling calm. I began to think about how the football players who struggled to remain on the team felt. Now I knew exactly how they felt. I began to think maybe this was a learning experience for me. It was clear to me I needed to work very hard to complete flight school not because I wanted to fly, but because I needed to grow from the experience of completing the challenge. In one way, I felt more pressure. I did feel much more confident in my ability to complete flight school.

The next four flights went well. I felt confident. When I talked with my roommate and other students, I was able to participate in sharing experiences. I started to feel like I was part of the team. I did my best to help my friends with ground school. Since we worked for ground school at our own pace, I was several lessons ahead of most of the students.

Then I went on my tenth flight, the check flight for the first solo. The first half of the session went well, but then the instructor changed the checkpoints for the navigation. The weather was terrible, but not bad enough to delay the flight. I had difficulty finding the checkpoints on the ground while we were flying. I missed two check points.

The instructor failed me on the flight. That meant I would stand before a Student Pilot Disposition Board and the board would probably drop me from flight school.

The Commanding Officer scheduled the Student Pilot Disposition Board on the morning of the second day after my failed flight. At first, I did my best to prepare for leaving flight school and facing the first significant failure of my life. As it turned out, I was able to use the two days to get ready for the meeting. The first night I was very depressed, but I began to have some confidence starting on the second morning.

I talked with a couple of the instructors I met. They told me to be confident and not to show signs of fear. I prayed again that night. I felt the same message as the night after the first failed flight. I realized I was preparing myself to face significant challenges later in my life. Again, I realized my goal was not to be a pilot. My goal was to overcome a considerable problem when my skills were not at the same level as the other students. I decided to let the board of officers know I had the character to finish the program. I may not have the skills of the other students, but I had been successful at every major endeavor I pursued.

I did not sleep the night before appearing before the board, but I did prepare as much as I could. I felt close to Jesus that night. By the end of the night, I was ready to do my best.

The next morning, I went to the administrative building. I was asked to wait in the hall. It was torture to sit as many other students walked past me. They all knew why I was there. The wait was over thirty minutes.

When I entered the room, I was asked to sit on a chair. There were three officers on the board. One of them explained all the reasons I was there. All three officers did their best to convince me it was in my best interest to leave flight school. They had several examples of flight students involved in serious accidents. They made it sound like they were doing me a favor by transferring me out of flight school.

After they finished reviewing all the details and the few options available to me, they asked me to discuss my point of view with them. I prepared my discussion so well that the message, "I can handle anything the board presented to me" was clear to all three of them.

After I explained that I worked very hard for the opportunity to attend flight school and was not open to the idea of quitting, I let them know the strength of my character and my desire to succeed would provide the direction I needed to succeed.

Then I looked at the senior officer on the board. I told him, "If you don't believe me, put on a helmet and fly with me this afternoon."

The senior officer asked me to wait in the hall again. After about ten minutes, the senior officer approached me and said, "We normally do not approve students with two failed flights to continue, but all three of us agree you have what it takes to be successful." Then I was told I had a check flight at 2:00 pm that afternoon. If I passed that flight, I would be back in the program.

I was so nervous. When I was alone, I prayed for one thing: to relax. I knew I had to be at my best. I could not afford to have any distractions. By the time I went to the flight line, I was completely relaxed and very confident.

The flight had no surprises. During previous sessions, I had performed every procedure the instructor asked. It was strange; I did not feel alone. Near the end of the flight, I did three touches and go patterns (flying in the traffic pattern at the runway, circling and touching the wheels, then taking off again). After the third touch and go, the instructor asked me to do a full stop. After I stopped the airplane on the runway, the instructor got out and told me to take off and fly for ten more minutes, then do a full landing.

I was shocked. I had never flown by myself. After the instructor left the plane, I taxied back to the runway and did a takeoff. It felt wonderful. At that point, I knew I would be successful and earn my wings.

When I returned to the runway and landed, the instructor met me back at the flight line. He gave me the paperwork that changed my status to active. I was so happy. I knew my faith and prayer allowed me to do my best when the pressure was applied.

At that point, I had only been in the flying part of flight school a week and a half. I had over a year to go, but I knew I would be successful. I did not feel the high level of stress for the rest of the program.

Although the instrument flying and night flying were much more challenging, I was comfortable. During the remaining flights, by far the most challenging for me was my first carrier landing (it was a solo flight). Even with the carrier landing, I did not feel the stress.

My First Child

After I finished the first three months of Flight School, my wife let me know she wanted to leave UCLA and come to be with me. She said her parents made it difficult for her. They asked her when she was going to leave me and get on with her life. I do not remember the actual words, but that was how I understood my wife's feelings.

I caught a flight back to California and met her there. We drove back to Pensacola, Florida again, and I continued Flight School.

My wife became pregnant shortly after her arrival at Pensacola. I still had almost a year of flight school remaining.

Everything went smoothly for the next nine months. Then, while I was on a long instrument check flight, my wife began her child labor. She was able to get her friend to drive her to the hospital. My wife was having challenges with the delivery.

When I arrived at the flight line after the check flight, the duty officer told me about the situation. I immediately called the hospital to ask about her status. They told me she was suffering.

I called my parents to let them know about the situation. My mother immediately went to LAX and caught a flight to Pensacola. That was amazing because back in 1974 there were few flights, especially to Pensacola, and they were costly. My parents did not have a lot of money. She flew to New Orleans and then caught a commuter flight to Pensacola. She arrived before my daughter, Jessica, was born.

My wife's labor lasted twenty-one hours. I was so worried about my wife's condition. At that time, fathers were not allowed in the delivery room. I had to wait all those hours, not knowing how my wife was doing.

My mother met me in the waiting room. I prayed for help. I had no power; I just had to wait. After a few hours, I relaxed, and somehow, I knew everything would be ok.

When my daughter was born, I was able to see her. That was a special moment. My wife chose her name, Jessica Kennedy Brandt. Kennedy was one of my wife's family names, and John Kennedy was my favorite President.

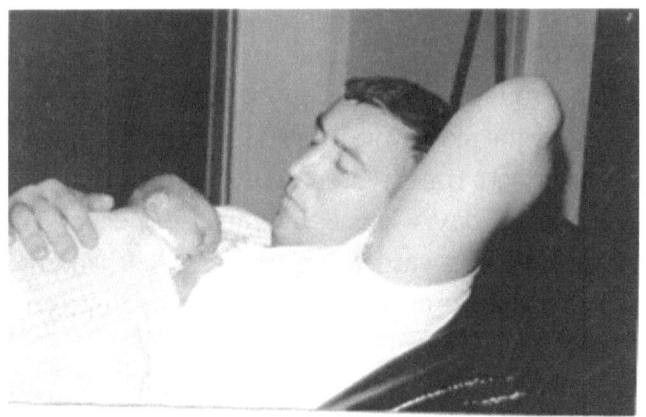

My Daughter Jessica One Week After Her Birth

I was so happy my wife was healthy. They kept me informed. I was surprised my mother could find the way to the hospital because it was an old single story building from World War II.

Jessica with Our Dog Walter

I was so grateful my mother supported us. She was always there when either my sister or I needed her.

My life was dramatically changed that day. I felt my life had meaning. Part of me would continue after I was gone. I was happy.

I finished ground school six months before I completed my flights. That gave me more time to spend with my wife and daughter. I also had much more time to prepare for the sessions.

It was a special day when I flew my final check flight. The Commanding Officer awarded me my wings. I had completed a second major challenge in my life. I was ready to prepare for the next challenge.

Marine Corps after Flight School

After earning my wings, I received orders to Southern California. All three of us drove to Orange County, California.

We spent some time settling in the area and searching for a house. We found one that was only four miles from the Marine Corps base. Homes were priced much lower back then. The purchase price was $27,500.

I was in a training squadron initially. Some of the students I knew from flight school were in the same squadron. There was a special bond because we all faced similar challenges, and all were successful.

I developed close relationships with several of the other pilots. In some ways, the training squadron was like flight school. There were instructors, and we had to fly specific instructional flights to qualify to operate in a specific aircraft.

There were significant differences from flight school; we were all certified pilots with official wings. We were expected to know how to: fly, navigate with instruments, and communicate with all the agencies. The training focus was on the specific capabilities of the aircraft. At the end of the training schedule, we were certified to fly that aircraft.

I had no issues with the training squadron. I graduated on time. The Wing Headquarters assigned me to a tactical group. Shortly after I left the training squadron, there was an accident in the training squadron, and four Marines died. I knew all the pilots involved. One of them survived. The accident was a mid-air collision above a mountain range in Orange County. The tactic they were practicing required them to fly a close formation low to the ground.

I remember thinking about how I had flown that tactic several times. I was nervous because we were flying so close to the other aircraft and we were near the ground; but I did not think it would end in a collision.

I was very depressed. The accident was the first of many casualties I would experience in the Marine Corps. One of the three aviators killed was my primary instructor in the training squadron. He was a great pilot with two tours in Vietnam.

Third Near-Death Experience

I was flying a helicopter from El Toro Marine Base in California to a training facility in 29 Palms, California. I had a crew of three in the aircraft with seven additional Marines as passengers. During the flight, the first stage hydraulic system failed. I could not control the air helicopter without a hydraulic system; the flight controls will not work. The aircraft has two hydraulic systems: first stage and second stage.

I reported the emergency to the flight controller on the radio. I was told to immediately change course to an Air Force base that was about twenty miles away.

I thought for a moment and felt a strong feeling something was not right. I told the air traffic controller the horses below me would move out of the way, and I was going to make an immediate landing. The controller argued with me for a moment but realized I was not changing the plan. I reduced power and pointed the helicopter toward an open field below. When we were about five hundred feet from the ground, the second stage hydraulic system failed, and I could no longer control the aircraft. We crashed in the middle of the horse ranch. Luckily it had been raining for three days, and the surface was soft. There were some significant injuries, but everyone survived.

I knew the Marine Corps was a dangerous profession, but that did not make my first air incident any better. I prayed and talked with the Chaplain, but I could not stop thinking about how I felt right before the crash, and that if I had tried to make it to the Air Force base, we would have all died.

Same Model Helicopter as the Accident

I met with my new Squadron Commander. He made it clear I had to get over the shock. He let me know we had classified missions scheduled in Asia. He told me I better be ready.

I knew it was not only my skill that kept me from being in similar accidents. The realization struck me that we must do our best and not be distracted by what might happen. I realized finishing flight school did not mean the pressure was off.

My faith allowed me to continue. I felt a purpose and I must do my best to fulfill that purpose.

Family Life Was Developing

Life at home was going well. I was working long hours but being at home was more stable than it had ever been. Jessica was walking and beginning to talk. That was exciting.

My wife loved riding horses. I remember one Saturday we watched the Belmont Stakes on TV. I never watch horse races, but I did this time because my wife told me it would be a unique race.

Secretariat won the triple crown. It was the first time it had happened in about 25 years. I was so happy to share the event with my wife. Jessica did not know what was happening, but she knew it was significant.

It felt good to have something so special happen outside the Marine Corps.

The other entertainment for me was watching Angels' baseball games. The team was not that good, but they had the best pitcher in the major league, Nolan Ryan. The stadium would only be half full during most games. When Nolan Ryan pitched, it was hard to get tickets. He was amazing.

It was nice to have a couple of releases from the preparation for war on the base.

I became confident with my flying. I began flying missions to support ground troops. All the lessons I learned playing football and struggling to make it through flight school were blessings now.

The concept of supporting the team, not my accomplishments was essential in this situation. I made sure I always tried to help everyone else be successful. I always thought about the importance of the squadron first.

Now, this is the third time the concept of supporting others was critical, and I still did not see the connection to the teachings I had about Jesus. Helping others is the very concept he taught. Why did it take me all these significant experiences to understand the source of the wisdom to overcome these stressful challenges? Now, when I think back to those times, it seems clear I should have read the Sermon on the Mount every time I faced a new major challenge. Jesus explains what to do.

My wife became pregnant again. This time she was supported by an excellent hospital. The Naval Hospital in Long Beach was a great facility.

Her pregnancy developed without incident. I was away on a classified mission out of the country when she began labor. I did not even know about the birth of my son until after he was born. At that time, communication was not as accessible as it is today; we had no personal email or cell phones.

The delivery went very well, and my wife was not in labor 21 hours like the first time. My wife told me the delivery took less than three hours. We named our new child Nathan Hollinger Brandt (Hollinger was my maternal grandfather's last name).

I felt terrible for not being there, but I was happy there were no complications, and everyone was healthy.

I was doing well in the tactical squadron for the first year. Then Jimmy Carter was elected President of the United States. Most of my fellow pilots thought this election would be good for us since Jimmy Carter graduated from the Naval Academy and served five years in the Navy.

We were all wrong. Jimmy Carter cut so much funding to the military; our squadron could only maintain two or three aircraft a day. The squadron had eighteen aircraft, but twelve or thirteen of them were down for maintenance at any given time. Only having a few aircraft available to fly on any given day made it unworkable. A pilot needs to fly about eighteen hours a month to maintain competence. We were only flying seven or eight hours a month because of the maintenance challenges. It was impossible to keep the squadron ready to respond to tactical situations.

Although the Marine Corps Air Wing had budget challenges, I wanted to make the Marine Corps a career. I was comfortable that my role was protecting people, not killing people, especially after being successful during flight school. I felt I worked hard and wanted to keep what I accomplished.

I had a four-year obligation after the completion of flight school. After the four-year commitment, the Marine Corps would release me from active duty.

I thought about the career opportunity in the Marine Corps and decided it was what I wanted to do. It would be a secure life for my family, and I would continue to grow as a pilot.

I prayed about the decision. I wanted to make the career decision, but I thought it might not be the choice I was supposed to make.

I talked to my squadron commander. He told me I had one option which was to apply for an upgrade in status to Active Duty Reserve Extended Duty. The Marine Corps would review all my records including every fitness report (official work review from my Commanding Officer).

I decided to apply for the upgrade in status. I submitted recommendations from all the senior officers I knew. I did my best to provide all the materials requested.

My application was approved. I was happy about my new status.

Fourth Near Death Experience

I was spending time with Jessica and Nathan at my wife's parent's house while my wife was with her parents away from home. I started to take a shower, and I heard Jessica screaming at the bathroom door.

I opened the door and saw her crying. She was only three years old at the time. She said Nathan was in the water. I grabbed her and ran to the backyard. Nathan was at the bottom of the pool.

I jumped in the water and pulled Nathan out. I struggled with his tongue because it was blocking his throat. I had to break his jaw so I could pull out his tongue. Then I kept giving him mouth to mouth breathing. He finally started to breathe.

The ambulance was going to take too long, so I picked up both Nathan and Jessica and ran to the hospital. It was about two miles away.

I did not pray, but I asked God for help on the way to the hospital. I did not get tired even though I was carrying both Nathan and Jessica. Nathan was breathing normally within half an hour. I was so relieved. I knew God was with me that day even though I did not formally pray.

Nathan would not take a bath for two years after that event, but he was healthy.

Change Jobs Within the Marine Corps

About two months after upgrading my status, the squadron had a regularly scheduled change of command. I was very close to my current squadron commander and was concerned he would be given an assignment overseas, and I would not be able to communicate with him regularly.

The new squadron commander had new ideas that helped us prepare for future missions. He did the best he could with the low budget. Each pilot still flew fewer than ten hours a month.

During my time in the tactical squadron, I worked well with all the crew at the flight line. I supported the team the best I could. This time I remembered the team concept. I made sure everything I did was for the benefit of the squadron and everyone in it.

Shortly after being transferred to the tactical squadron, the Marine Corps promoted me to Captain. Being a captain was essential for me because my father did not consider me a real officer until I was a captain. He was so excited when he heard about the promotion. I sent him my official commission document with the rank of Captain on it. He was thrilled when I graduated from flight school, but when I became a Captain, he felt I made it. It no longer mattered to him that I was in the Marine Corps instead of the Army.

However, my new squadron commander did not share my commitment to the entire team. He made it clear to me I was not to become familiar with enlisted personnel (everyone who was not an officer). He told me that the rank structure in the Marine Corps was absolute.

This approach to enlisted staff was a significant challenge for me. The crew that supported my aircraft was critical to me. It was difficult not to have a conversation with my team. There were things I could do for them like complement them for work well done and do what I could to make their job easier.

This entire situation created a significant challenge for me. I clearly understood the rank structure. I was taught about it during Officer Candidate School and again in the Basic School for new officers. It did make sense that if an officer is making life and death decisions in combat, that officer should not have personal relationships with the people they command.

Learning the concept in a class is different than living it in a tactical squadron. In the air wing, the pilot and the crew are a close team. I depend on them to make sure the aircraft is ready to fly. My life depends on the quality of their work. It was tough for me not to be friends with the crew that supported me.

I did my best to satisfy the requirements of the Marine Corps and still commit to my Christian faith. I loved flying, and I loved being a part of the Marine Corps. It was difficult for me to consider that a career in the Marine Corps may not work for me.

I was not against the rules of the Marine Corps, but I was not sure those rules would work for me. I could not believe I was considering not making the Marine Corps a career after working so hard to earn my wings and change my active duty status.

I decided not to make any decisions until I had adjusted to the new commander and had more understanding about how life in the Marine Corps would work. I had only spent a little under two years in the tactical squadron at this time.

Life in the squadron was workable for the next six months. I developed working relationships with the crew personnel within the rules, yet I maintained my effort to work hard to help everyone, not work for my credit.

After the six months passed, I began to feel stronger that a career in the Marine Corps was not what I was supposed to do. This thought caused me stress. Every time I prayed for guidance, I felt more uncomfortable with my situation.

I could not talk with the other pilots because they would never understand how I was feeling. They all loved the Marine Crops and were not concerned about the rules.

As I thought about my situation, a message came to me. One reason I was uncomfortable was not because of the rules or not being able to have friendships with enlisted personnel. The idea was that a career in the Marine Corps was not what I was supposed to do. I learned about facing challenges, supporting people, and operating under stress. My entire experience in the Marine Corps prepared me to meet and complete other challenges.

Working through the challenges in Basic School, then applying them to flight school, being accepted to flight school, and then completing flight school all prepared me for the next phase in my life.

I felt right about this conclusion, but I was not sure what to do with the final two years of my obligation. Continuing to focus on flying in the squadron was not going to advance me in the direction I needed to go.

I studied other options within the Marine Corps. I loved flying and wanted to continue. I did not find any positions available to me that would help me advance in the direction I wished to go. I was not even sure what that direction was.

I did pray for guidance and continued to think about options. Then my former squadron commander called me and asked me to meet him for lunch.

When we met for lunch, he asked me how I was doing. I told him about my challenges with the rules but also told him I was able to follow those rules.

Then he asked me if I would like to transfer out of the tactical squadron and work for him at the Wing Headquarters. I could not believe the timing of his question. However, I did want to continue flying as long as I was on active duty in the Marine Corps.

I asked him about the job. He told me he had been assigned to command the technology support for the Third Marine Air Wing in El Toro. He wanted me to be his deputy.

I told him I still wanted to fly. He told me I could even fly eight to twelve hours a month, but it would be with a different squadron. I told him I was not sure. Then he asked me what I wanted to do with the rest of my life.

I was struggling with that question myself. By this time, I knew I was ready to begin a new challenge where I would develop new talent. I wanted to work with people and promote services or products that help people.

I talked to him about some of these ideas. He said we were in the mid-seventies and the world was changing. He said technology was going to be a significant part of everyone's life during the next generation.

He told me if I wanted a challenge, I should consider technology. He described it as demanding like flying, except it would affect everyone. Then he said if I agreed to work under him, he would send me to the computer science school in Quantico, Virginia. The school was only three months, but it was intense. I would spend the next two years supporting and implementing technology for the entire Third Marine Air Wing.

I decided to make the change. I moved to my new office within a week. I had a staff who helped me with the administrative part of the job.

I had no idea how great this opportunity was for me. Like similar situations in my past, I thought to leave the tactical squadron was going to be a tremendous loss. It was the same as leaving Paradise or not becoming part of the Infantry in the Marine Corps.

Two weeks after returning from the Technology School in Quantico, I was working at the same pace as flight school. My job had several primary responsibilities.

The first responsibility was to interface with all technology companies who wished to sell software or equipment to the Third Marine Air Wing. This task allowed me to have relationships with IBM, Univac, Hewlett Packard, and many other companies.

The second responsibility was to interface between the Third Marine Air Wing and the data center (it was called the Fourth FASC). The Fourth FASC had many software developers and technicians. I developed several friendships that would continue after I left active duty. I did everything I could to help them, and they all supported me.

The third responsibility was to create the slide presentation the Third Marine Air Wing Commanding General would deliver to the President of the United States. The Commanding General gave the presentation twice a year. President Nixon would come to Southern California twice a year and stay at his home in San Clemente. He would always visit the El Toro Marine base to receive the Third Marine Air Wing Readiness presentation. I had to work with the commanders of all the groups to define the slides. I also worked with the photo department to create the physical slides. Then I would deliver the presentation to the Chief of Staff. After the Chief of Staff made changes, I would have the photo lab create new slides. Working with the photo lab was a critical job. More importantly, I learned many new skills. I had to work with hundreds of people to create the presentation. There could be no mistakes.

Within a few weeks, I realized with the help of prayer; I did make the right decision. This new job was a fantastic opportunity to grow in so many ways. Again, I thought I would be making a significant sacrifice leaving the tactical squadron, just like when I left Paradise. The message from prayer allowed me to be comfortable with the decision to leave the tactical squadron. It was not until about six months later I realized it was the right decision. Then five years later, I knew the decision completely changed the direction of my life and allowed me to develop new skills.

In those last two years in the Marine Corps, I learned much more about technology than I learned about government in the four years of college.

Developing a relationship with IBM was key to my future. IBM made monthly presentations to me regarding the latest mainframe and minicomputer advancements. I scheduled and attended meetings with the group commanders and IBM to review system advancements.

It is hard to believe, but back then there were no personal computers, fax machines, and very few copy machines. Xerox had the patent on copy machines at that time. The Third Marine Air Wing only had one copy machine on the entire base when I started my new position. By the time I left active duty, the Wing had several.

The job of creating the command brief for the President required my attention all the time because it took the full six months between summaries to develop the presentation. I developed a close relationship with all the group and squadron commanders.

It was a challenge to develop a relationship with the group and squadron commanders to document all the updated information. Working with the Chief of Staff to create the presentation was a significant effort. My communication skills, organizational understanding, and creative ability developed at a swift pace.

Everyone I supported from the Third Marine Air Wing command staff was very professional, but they all had their view regarding what was necessary.

Years later this experience was critical when I developed business relationships with major corporations.

Probably the most valuable experience was working with the Fourth FASC to support the technology for the Third Marine Air Wing. I developed close relationships with the most talented technology people.

One year before leaving active duty, a partnership was formed during off-duty hours to create a new company. We knew personal computers would be available within another two years. We worked during off-hours to plan the software we would develop, and we selected the computer hardware we would use to promote our products. Because of my relationship with key people at IBM and Hewlett Packard, we were able to access the information we needed to get started.

One of the partners was a Major in the Marine Corps. He not only supported the technology requirements of the tactical organizations, but he was an accountant as well. His background was a valuable part of our partnership.

The other partner was a software developer. He understood what to develop, and he had the skills to build software himself and later to manager developers. Both partners had excellent communication skills, which was critical.

I was the one with no formal training. My responsibility was to develop a base of customers. Within six months, I identified our first customer. I only had one more year on active duty. The customer was a promoter of motorcycle races in sports stadiums across the United States. They required a unique accounting system to manage the business.

We had to assemble hardware as well. At that time, there were no acceptable small computers. I had a relationship with Hughes Aircraft because of my duties with the Third Marine Air Wing. I met with a circuit board developer. We purchased an operating chip from Digital Research and then paid the Hughes Aircraft developer to create a circuit board with the operating chip on it.

Then we purchased memory boards from Digital Research. We hired a company that made furniture to make a cabinet that stored the circuit boards inside, and we placed the printer on top. We put the monitor on a separate table.

We put the keyboard on a tray located under the monitor. We pulled out the tray when we wanted to use the keyboard.

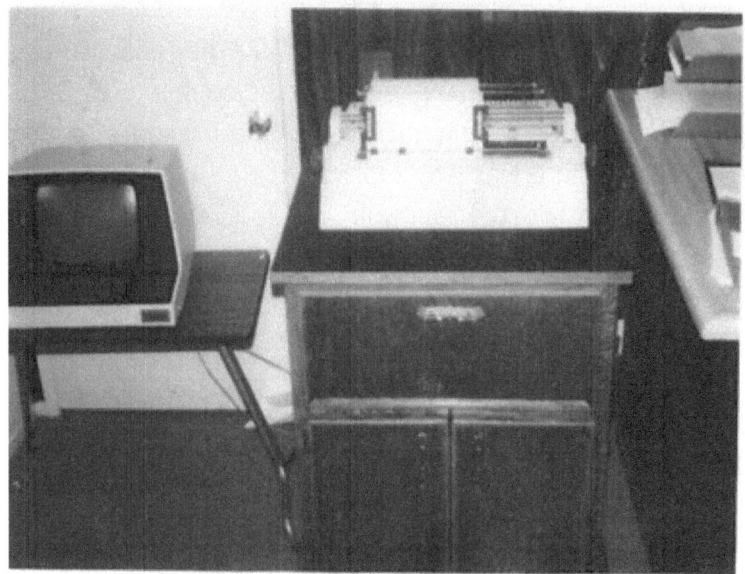

Our First Computer with Printer and Monitor

I traveled to Monterey, California, to meet with Gary Kildall, the owner of Digital Research. The CP/M (Computer Program/ Manager) Operating System was the only choice we had to develop our application. Digital Research was very cooperative during the meeting. They were willing to help our company launch our first product.

We wanted to use the Basic Language. Digital recommended I call Bill Gates from Microsoft and discuss their Basic Language. My trip to Monterey was a couple of years before Bill Gates had a conflict with Gary Kildall about IBM.

I called Bill Gates, who was in New Mexico at the time. He did make a trial version of Microsoft's Basic Language available to me.

Our team worked with the language for a couple of months. We had a lot of issues with the language at the time. There were some technical issues, but the main challenge was that it was interpretive. Interpretive meant the source code was embedded in the code we would sell to customers. Not only did this make our development code public, but the processing was slow.

I went back to Digital Research to discuss our challenge with the Basic Language from Microsoft. They told me they had just finished the beta version of a new language called Commerce Basic. They compiled the code, so we did not have to ship the source code with the application, and it was much faster.

We were happy with the test results and decided to use Commercial Basic.

It was a significant effort to form a new company while all three of us were still active duty in the Marine Corps. Sometimes we worked all night at the client's office since we could not work during the day. There was no internet for the general public back then, so we had to do a lot of the testing and some of the development work at the customer's office.

I was released from the Marine Corps a few months after we started the business.

CHAPTER 6

STARTING A BUSINESS

I Was the Only Full-Time Partner

We started the new company in September of 1978. I worked out of my home in the beginning. My wife and I purchased a home in Riverside about one year before I left the Marine Corps.

My daughter Jessica was old enough to run and talk. Before leaving the Marine Corps, I loved arriving home after work. Jessica would run through the house to see me. We were very close.

About a year into the new business, Jessica started running with me. There was a high school close to our house. Jessica, Nathan, and I would walk to the track on the school property. Jessica and I would run around the track and Nathan would run across the middle of the field and meet us every half lap. Sometimes Nathan would fall while he was running. He would laugh and get back up. Those were great times.

Bob Decker graduated from Perdue University in computer science. While in the Marine Corps, he developed significant software for the Marine Corps. He was a First Lieutenant at the Fourth FASC.

The other partner, Major Jim Ray, was the accountant. He could define projects and document workflows. Software development was not his expertise, but he did his share.

Bob Decker worked long hours because he frequently worked ten-hour shifts with the Marine Corps and then worked all night at the client's office. He did a great job. Bob was gifted because he could listen to the customer directly and create the code to support customer requirements. Years later, I learned how few people have that ability.

None of us had business experience. There were many challenges in the first six months. There were times when I had doubt about our ability to grow the business. My challenge was that I was the only one the prospects saw until they were close to making the buying decision. Both Bob Decker and Jim Ray helped every way they could, but since both were still on active duty, I was the front end of the business. There were times when I doubted our ability to grow the business.

Initial Start Was Positive

The business started very well. The developer, Bob Decker, was talented. During the first six months of the business; we closed sales with several customers. There was enough business for us to keep going. At that time, the challenge was a lack of computer software or computer hardware distribution. Computer stores did not exist, but some software companies advertised in the two computer magazines that existed. Our only marketing was me calling companies directly.

We charged about $40,000 per customer. That was a lot of money at the time, but there was no competition. I found small companies that could not afford to hire enough staff to take care of the billing, paying bills, managing the accounting, and generating new business. We helped them in all those areas.

Opportunity Within Marine Corps

Although I was able to identify some prospects, the long-term vision of the business was uncertain.

After the first four months, I was not feeling as confident as I originally thought. One of my previous commanding officers called me and let me know I could go back to active duty if I desired.

I was unsure of what to do. I prayed about the situation because I had no confidence the prospective customers would be open to automating. I knew the company would grow eventually, but I was concerned about compensating the other two partners when they left active duty.

I am not sure if it was a dream or whether God answered my prayer by providing clarity. After about a week, it became clear to me I was not participating in this business to become wealthy or even financially comfortable. I was in the company to develop the experience and understanding of the marketplace. I made contacts I would use the rest of my life.

I knew I would be comfortable for the rest of my life if I returned to the Marine Corps. I loved flying, I traveled all over the world, my wife embraced the routines of an officer's wife, and I liked the Marine Corps itself.

However, I still had the challenge that I was not a good fit for the Marine Corps because of the regulations about not becoming friends with enlisted personnel. My second challenge was that my entire life, God made it clear the correct decision was the one that helped me develop in a specific direction. I moved from flying to technology even though I liked flying; I had no interest in technology initially. By this time, I had learned to question my feelings regarding major life direction decisions to identify what was best for me over a long period.

After one week of thinking about it, I felt firm. I let my former commanding officer know I was not going back to the Marine Corps, but I wished him well.

Shortly after deciding to stay with the business, I felt I was developing my entire experience to address significant challenges in my future. I was not sure how this experience would relate, but I did understand I needed both the contacts and the business experience. I also used my Christian teaching to address business challenges. I was amazed at how advice from the New Testament applied to business.

Back to Business

I mentioned earlier that our first customer was Stadium Motor Sports, a nationwide promoter of motorcycle races. I met many essential contacts from that business relationship. The other advantage was that I learned a lot about business. That owner did not have any financial experience, but he knew every detail about his business. The lesson learned from working with him helped me many times throughout my business career.

Our second customer was a highly successful realtor who focused on rental income properties. The owner had many great business ideas. At that time, there were no spreadsheet software applications. I worked with him to develop software that analyzed a potential investment for five years. It calculated the forecasted internal rate of return for each year and the final numbers at the end of five years. The calculation allowed up to five loans. The strategy was brilliant. We developed software that included the purchase price of the property, up to five loans with detailed payment terms, the current property value, the forecasted property value, and forecasted expenses.

What made the strategy so brilliant was that the application was used to purchase property, not sell it. The realtor would find an apartment building he wished to purchase. Then he would use the software to create his offer. He would always enter the seller's asking price as the cost. Then he would include several loans with different payment terms. He would continue to change the payment terms on the loans until the application showed a minimum of 25%

internal rate of return for the entire investment. The seller almost always accepted the offer because it would be for the asking price.

The problem with this application is that we thought we would be able to sell it to other realtors, but this customer did not cooperate. His lawyer told us the realtor paid us to develop the software which meant he owned the code and we could not sell it to other companies.

I learned from that experience. I realized we should sell the use of the software, not the application itself. A few years later, everyone sold software that way. We had no experience to predict that happening. I did develop a close relationship with an attorney from church for all future business transactions.

The third customer was Oakley, the sunglass company. They were a fantastic customer. At the time we worked with them, they only had eight employees and one warehouse. I developed many business skills while working with them.

We gradually developed more business and began to grow. The new company had progressed through the startup phase. There were more challenges to come.

CHAPTER 7

MARRIAGE BREAKUP

The Actual Split

My life went through many changes after leaving Paradise in my junior year of high school. During the first sixteen years of my experience, I lived in small towns in Northern California, where everyone knew each other. Then I abruptly moved to Los Angeles, where the lifestyle is different. I was married while only nineteen years old. I adjusted to college life with work, football, a wife, and course work. The Marine Corps was a completely different type of experience. Finally starting a small business with two partners was another life change.

After I left active duty in the Marine Corps in 1978, I became unhappy with my marriage. I am not sure what was the main reason. It was my fault. My wife was supportive of the Marine Corps even though she did not approve of the Vietnam War, and she did not blame the Marine Corps for her not studying in Russia. She was terrific with the children. In my opinion, she changed significantly for the better (she was not as judgmental) since we married. She was much friendlier with our friends. She always treated me with respect, and she supported all my decisions regarding career choices.

I struggled with knowing I was unhappy for a few months. All the details are not appropriate for this book, but I do not think my wife was the reason I was unhappy with the marriage.

I did not approach this decision in the same way I approach the other life changing decisions. I focused on being unhappy and let that feeling drive me.

I am not saying I made the wrong decision. I am saying I did not approach it with an open mind and pray for guidance. When looking back on that time, I think leaving the marriage may have been the correct decision, but I mishandled it. I did not consider the other factors as I did with all the different life-altering choices. I regretted the way I handled the marriage break up for the rest of my life.

My wife did not want to break up the marriage, but she never tried to make things difficult for me. When the marriage broke up, I moved out and stayed with one of my customers for a few months.

The children lived with my wife in the beginning. She not only took care of them but in some cases, she would drive them to where I was so I could spend time with them.

At first, I still had a strong relationship with Jessica, my eldest child. She was six years old at that time. She would call me and let me know how she was doing. A few years later she called me to ask me to buy a TV for them. I bought them a TV that week and took it to them the following weekend. My wife told me not to leave the TV with them. She felt that the small TV they had was all they needed.

I felt bad for Jessica, but I should have asked my wife before I made the purchase. A couple of years after that, Jessica asked me to take Nathan on a trip so Jessica could have a birthday party with her friends.

When it came time for the divorce to be final, my wife was extremely cooperative. She told me to have my lawyer create the agreement, and she would sign it. She did not want any money. She wanted me to purchase a house near her parent's house and let her live in it rent-free with the children.

I agreed. I felt so awful about myself. My wife was as Christian as one could be without being a Christian. She deserved better than she received from me.

Family Life After the Marriage Breakup

I spent time with my children for about two weekends a month. Since they lived in Santa Clarita, California, I bought season passes to Magic Mountain for the three children and myself. We spent lots of time at Magic Mountain. The children enjoyed Magic Mountain for several years.

Their mother helped them participate with youth sports programs. All three of them joined. I would do my best to be there for their games. It was a little awkward because my wife's parents would also attend the games. However, her parents never made me feel uncomfortable.

One year Jessica's team won the championship for her age group. They all enjoyed playing. I appreciated their mother doing the work to support them with their extra activities.

I did appreciate that my former wife let me know about all the activities, including the softball games. It meant so much to be there when they played. All three were excited about the opportunity.

Sports were always important to me, so I was happy to support my children's efforts to play.

I made sure I never expressed a desire for them to do anything I did. I wanted their future to be their own choice like it was for me.

Jessica

Nathan

Jessica during a Softball Game

Nathan during a Baseball Game

I took the children to church on Sundays at the Grace Community Church in Sun Valley, California. It was a fantastic church; the Pastor was John MacArthur. The church had a large campus with several buildings. It had fifteen thousand people attend each service. They had a full orchestra and a large choir.

Jessica and I went to the primary service. The other two children went to the children's service in another building. I was so grateful to their mother for cooperating. I do believe my children benefited from attending church. It was vital for them to know what I thought without forcing my beliefs on them.

CHAPTER 8

TRAVELING WITH MY CHILDREN

Spend Time with Nathan

My first wife called me and told me she had concerns about Nathan. This call was during the summer of 1984 when Nathan was nine years old. She felt that Nathan needed to spend one on one time with me. My first wife mentioned that he spent most of his family time with women or girls; his sisters, his mother, and his grandmother. I was grateful again that my first wife was thoughtful and shared her concerns with me.

I was deeply concerned. I wanted to help Nathan but was not sure what to do. I prayed for help but did not feel strongly about a specific answer. The feeling I had was to call my first wife and ask her what she thought would help. As it turned out, that was the answer.

When I called my first wife and asked her what she thought would help, she told me I needed to spend enough time one on one with him to help him feel good about himself.

I thought about that. I could see how Nathan would be uncomfortable without direct attention from his father. When I talked with him, he was not sure why he felt uneasy.

I thought about the situation for a couple of days. Then I felt confident I knew what to do. I had a dream where I was spending time with Nathan by himself. We were doing things that boys typically do. He laughed and looked happy during the vision.

After considering the options, I knew I needed to do something with Nathan that would give him more male influence. I decided to take him on a weekend backpacking trip at one of the local mountains. I already had backpacking gear; I just needed to purchase a pack for Nathan.

Nathan never had that type of adventure. We planned the trip for two weekends later.

When we went on the trip, Nathan loved it at first. When we were about one-third of the way up the mountain, he began to complain. I felt a need to be firm. He needed to accomplish something that would make him proud. I told him to quit winning and keep hiking. He continued to complain for the next twenty minutes. I felt he had to be successful. I silently prayed for help.

A few minutes later, a condor flew right over us. The condor flew so low we were both almost hit. Nathan was so excited. Then the condor flew to the top of the mountain. Nathan followed quickly. The condor was resting on a limb of one of the trees up on top. When we made it to the top of the mountain, Nathan knew he accomplished something extraordinary. The trip had met its objective. Nathan felt good about himself.

Nathan and I On His First Hike

After reflecting on the trip, I realized it probably was not that he needed to do something male-oriented, he needed to feel special. During the next fifteen years, I took Nathan backpacking all over the world. I also took my daughters on trips to other countries, but they chose to stay in hotels and take trains instead of hiking. I believe that I understood God's message and it made a difference for all my children.

A Camping Trip with the Children

The next year I took all three of my children camping on a local mountain. It was a great experience. All three of the children had fun the entire time. They played games and told stories around the campfire.

The trip went fine until the early evening when the rangers warned us that a bear was in the area. I had the children help me move all the food to the car. Then we talked about it. All the other campers left.

I had gone bear hunting with my grandfather when I was young. I still remember what he told me, "Sometimes you get the bear, and sometimes the bear gets you." He told me never to challenge a bear. Just keep my distance, and everything will be OK.

We did not see the bear, but all three of the children had a new story to tell. I felt close to all three of them. The experience did help me connect with my daughters.

Additional Hikes in California With Nathan

During the next couple years, Nathan and I went on a few hiking trips in other parts of California. Every time was special. During the hikes we had great views from the mountains and along the rivers. We saw several large waterfalls.

About one year after our first hiking trip, we went to a mountain in Northern California. I had not been there since I was a child. We spent a week hiking and camping.

I felt close to God when we were hiking. That was especially true on this trip. It was cold as we climbed up the mountain. At one-point Nathan said, "Jesus must have been cold when he was hiking." I was so surprised when he thought of that. It was like we were both thinking along the same track.

Before we began the hike, I took Nathan to Hayfork, the town where I was born. We went to the store my grandfather owned when I was a child. I felt very close to God when we walked into the store. It had changed a lot since I was a child, or my memory was not accurate. Going to Hayfork was a great beginning to the trip.

Nathan had no challenges with the hike. I remember him throwing rocks in the river when we started. We spent three days hiking up the mountain. The view at the top was terrific. It felt good to create the campsite every night with the tent. We had plenty of food. Then we spent two more days going down the mountain and back to where we started.

After camping, we drove to my grandparent's house and spent the night. It was nice to see them. I felt great about the entire trip.

I was grateful for the original spiritual message to take Nathan on these trips. This trip was a little longer than the last one, but Nathan knew what to expect, and he was a year older. I knew the trips would help both of us the rest of our lives.

We continued to go on trips over the next several years. We made one more hiking and camping trip locally. Then we started traveling to different parts of the world.

South American Trip with Nathan

Our first international trip was to South America in 1991. Nathan was in college by the time we began this trip. We scheduled it during his spring break. We flew to Santiago, Chile. Then we took an antique train (from 1910) to the southern tip of Chile. From there we hiked over the Andes to Argentina. It was a terrific hike, although we did not see another human being during the six days. There were giant waterfalls, deep canyons, and many types of birds. This hike had its challenges because of the elevation, but we both did well.

Nathan Beside the Antique Train

It was nice to spend time together without other people. We had enough food. I purchased it from a sporting goods store before leaving. When we were near the top of the mountain pass, I felt like I was close to God. The air was thin, but the birds and the waterfalls made the event spectacular.

We lost a day of hiking because I thought we checked in at the immigration office, but it was not the correct location. We lost a day because we had to go back to check-in at the right place.

Beginning of the Chile/Argentina Hike

Waterfall on the Andes Mountains

We hiked back to Chile and took a bus to Santiago where we caught our flight home. We spent one night in a hotel before flying home.

Trip to Europe With Jessica

In 1995, Jessica was on her spring break from school. We flew from Los Angeles to London for the start of the trip. We only spent one full day in London, but we managed to see many of the main sites.

We stayed at the London Hilton Hotel. It was located right in the heart of London. It was close to the main sites.

We Walked to Buckingham Palace

We walked to most of the sites. The city was beautiful.

Jessica in London

As you can see from the picture, we were cold because the temperature was lower than in Southern California.

After spending the day in London, we had dinner in the city and then returned to the hotel.

Everything was perfect except one thing, that night there was a one-hour time change, and we did not know about it. We almost missed our flight to Rome. I was so stressed. I prayed several times silently. We did make it to the airport just in time. I was so relieved. I wanted this trip to be extraordinary for Jessica.

After a short flight, we stayed at the Hilton Hotel in Rome. It was on a hill that overlooked the city of Rome. The hotel was about forty-five minute cab ride from the airport. We saw several extraordinary sites as we went through Rome. The hotel was spectacular. We had a suite that overlooked the swimming pool and the city of Rome. The room itself was the nicest I had ever experienced.

We spent a little time planning our three days in Rome. We organized the sites we wanted to see and talked about what parts of Rome we would visit for each of the three days.

I had a detailed travel guide which provided the information we needed for the planning of all the cities on this trip.

Shortly after checking into the hotel and reviewing the travel guide, we caught a cab to the central part of Rome and began our adventure.

View from the Balcony of the Hotel

We went to the Vatican first. There were long lines to see most of the main sites. We had the whole day, so it was not an issue.

We enjoyed visiting Vatican City. We had seen pictures and videos, but this was different. We had to wait over two hours to see the Sistine Chapel; the wait was worth it. It is hard to imagine how Michelangelo spent four years upside down painting this beautiful ceiling.

Sistine Chapel

While in the Chapel, I felt a strong spiritual feeling. I was surprised because there were so many people in the chapel and several distractions. Although I was not a Catholic, I did know I was in a holy place.

Touring the central part of Vatican City was an incredible experience. I could feel the history that goes back two thousand years.

We spent the next two days visiting the main sites in Rome. There were so many sites to see.

Vatican City

Although the main areas in Vatican City are two thousand years old, they still look beautiful. I was amazed. I was happy Jessica was able to experience all the history.

The other significant sites in Rome were spectacular as well, but they were not as preserved as Vatican City.

One of the primary sites was the Colosseum. The weather over all those years had damaged the site, but the city preserved it. We walked through most of the structure.

Roman Colosseum

It was not difficult to visualize how it looked two thousand years ago. I envisioned how unique the site was for all the Roman citizens.

We walked through many of the other major historical sites. I had no problem visualizing how the Roman Senate met to discuss major military campaigns.

Jessica Walking Toward the Ruins

We spent the second and third days in Rome visiting all the ruins. It was an adventure to see the sites we studied in school.

The three days in Rome went quickly for us. We took the train from Rome to the beautiful city of Florence. After arriving at Florence, we viewed Florence from a ridge that surrounded the city.

There is a cathedral in the center of the city that was built over five hundred years ago, but was still beautiful. Of course, we went to the Statue of David. It was great to see the statue in person. We had no idea how detailed the figure was until we were close to it.

Statue of David

Then we rode the train to Venice. Because of the water channels, it was very different than any other city we visited. Some people told us if we went to Florence in the summer, the smell from the water would be substantial. It was not an issue when we were there.

A Water Channel Inside Venice

We stayed in Venice for two days. The time we spent on the boats was incredible. We will always remember the unique city surrounded by water.

From Venice, we traveled by train to Paris. Of course, Paris was beautiful.

We viewed the significant sites of Paris as well as the Louvre museum. We spent time at the Notre Dame Cathedral.

Notre Dame Cathedral

While in Paris we traveled to the Palace of Versailles. The estate and the palace were much larger and more complex than we expected. We did the tour inside and walked through the grounds.

Jessica Walking Toward the Palace

After our stay in Paris, we went to Yugoslavia. The date of the trip was before the Soviet Union fell so, we were behind the Iron Curtin. I silently thanked God that everything went well, and Jessica experienced a completely different culture.

After Yugoslavia, we went to Germany and flew home from there.

This entire trip was exceptional. Although we did not hike or camp, both of us grew closer to each other. The trip fulfilled the same purpose as the hiking fulfilled for Nathan and me. I thanked God for helping me find the resources to make the trip, and more importantly, sending me the original message that helped me reach my children. I felt so much closer to Jessica.

Trip to Greece With My Daughter

In 1996, we flew to London for two days and then flew to Greece. We were able to see places in London we did not see on the earlier trip. We visited Westminster Abbey, Parliament and some of the surrounding countryside.

We also ate lunch at the original Hardrock Cafe, where we saw Beatles pictures, guitars, and other memorabilia on the walls. It was an excellent experience for both of us. The Beatles were my favorite rock group.

We flew from London to Athens. The trip to Greece is the only trip I took outside of the United States, where I rented a car and drove to all the locations. When we arrived in Athens, we were able to get the rental car right away. However, we tried to use the maps they gave us to find our way to the hotel. I was driving. We were lost almost immediately.

After about an hour of driving, we discovered that we needed to go to a different part of the city to reach the hotel. We did arrive after another hour.

Athens was amazing. There were ruins right in the middle of the city. We were able to walk through most of them.

Downtown Athens

We spent two days in Athens. There were so many places to see. On the third day, we took a bus to Delphi.

It took half the day to get to Delphi. It is a fantastic place at the top of the mountain. There is one narrow road that leads up the way to the town. The road was so thin that when a bus approached us from the other direction, there were only a couple of inches between the two coaches. One bus had to stop, and the other one took twenty minutes to pass because it had to go so slowly.

When we arrived at the top, it was beautiful. There was a view of the entire valley below. We saw the ancient City of Thieves from the top.

We went to an outdoor theater. We sat on the same seat Alexander the Great sat when he talked with the religious leaders about invading Persia.

We both felt how unique Delphi was. We ate lunch at a restaurant with a view of the entire valley 4,000 feet below.

The Greeks Built the buildings into the mountain. It almost looked like the buildings were carved directly from the mountain. We could tell they were thousands of years old, but they were completely functional.

After we ate lunch, the bus took us back to our hotel.

Delphi Near the Theater Where We Sat

Restaurant with a View of the Valley

Theater Where Alexander the Great Sat

After spending the night in the hotel, we drove the next day to Olympia. Olympia was special. I always wanted to see the site of the first Olympic Games.

This time we did not get lost. We stayed in a beautiful hotel on a hill overlooking the original Olympic site. There was a museum that had mock pictures of what the village looked like over two thousand years ago. Athletes stayed there for one-year training before they competed. Each athlete was an individual; they did not represent a country like the Olympic Games of today. We walked through the areas where they lived and where they trained.

There was no large stadium. It was just a simple running track. The people who watched the event sat on the side of a hill. I was fascinated.

We got up early in the morning and walked through the entire site all by ourselves. Two hours later a bus full of tourists arrived. We were amazed that we had private access to one of the wonders of the world for over two hours.

The Olympic Stadium

We spent the second day in the small town of Olympia. It only had three streets but had lots of stores selling souvenirs. We purchased several items. I still have some of them today.

The next morning, we drove the rented car to Nafplio. Nafplio was the capital of Greece in the 1800s. It is located right next to the ocean. We stayed in a hotel with windows that opened. The street below had a restaurant that put tables on the road in the evening. We enjoyed eating dinner there.

Nafplio

After two days in Nafplio, we caught a boat to three of the Greek islands.

Ruins on One of the Greek Islands

The ruins were incredible. We walked inside them. We were amazed that not many people were there. It was easy to imagine what they were like when built. The marble was beautiful.

After spending two days on the islands, we drove back to Athens and then flew home via London.

Trip to Europe With Nathan

In 1997 I took my next trip with Nathan in Europe. Nathan had a good friend from high school who was already in Europe. We met him in Norway. During this trip, we did not hike or camp, but we did do a lot of walking.

We spent the first two days in Norway. It was beautiful. I was happy for Nathan to experience a new culture. He did experience some culture in Chile, but we were alone most of the time on the hiking trail.

We went to Lillehammer where Lillehammer hosted the Winter World Olympics. What a beautiful place. We were amazed at how small the town of Lillehammer was. There were only a few streets.

Everyone there seemed happy. We knew we were in a place that we would remember.

Nathan and His Friend Jeff At Lillehammer

Our next stop was Sweden. Each of the cities we visited had a unique culture. People were friendly to us in all the towns. The following location we visited was the city of Stockholm. The town was over one thousand years old.

I thanked God for sending me the message to make these trips. I knew Nathan was experiencing things he could not do any other way. Nathan was happy the whole time in Sweden. It was amazing seeing some of the buildings that dated back one thousand years.

Nathan and Jeff In Stockholm

After our stay in Sweden, we caught a cruise to Finland. We stayed on the ship overnight. The night was an experience because we roamed through the passages and talked with people from all over Europe. The scenery was fantastic.

Nathan In Helsinki, Finland

After arriving in Finland, we went to the stadium where Finland hosted the 1952 Summer Olympics. It was an abandoned stadium.

We walked across the field. It was not maintained very well. It was still lovely to stand at the same place where Finland conducted the Summer Olympic Games.

Stadium in Finland

We went to a mall and purchased a few items. The mall was like shopping centers in America. Traveling within the city was easy; we experienced no challenges using buses or trains. We were very comfortable in the hotel. We did use the steam room. We watched the NCAA Basketball finals in the hotel room which UCLA won the tournament. We both liked UCLA so that added value to the trip.

We walked around Helsinki to view the city. It was beautiful. The people were friendly and seemed happy. We both enjoyed being there, although it was cold and had lots of snow.

We had a great dinner and then began to think about our train ride the next day to Russia.

We left on the train the next morning for St. Petersburg. What a difference. It was even colder than Finland, 10 degrees below zero. As we traveled through the city, everyone seemed to be wearing dark-colored clothes and looked unhappy. It was very depressing.

Then we went to the Hermitage Museum. It was the best museum I have ever seen, including the Louvre in Paris. There were fantastic art exhibits. One room only had Rembrandt paintings.

Nathan In Front of the Hermitage Museum

We were surprised when we entered the museum; we paid the admission for both of us, and they required a separate admission fee for my camera. That was a first for us.

Nathan Inside the Hermitage Museum

We spent a full day walking through the museum and did not see all of it. That day made our stay in St. Petersburg worthwhile.

After we left the Hermitage Museum, we began walking toward the hotel. The snow was falling, and we were so cold we could hardly walk. Our map described the locations in English, but all the street signs were in Russian. After about twenty minutes, we did not know where we were. No one spoke English, and there were no signs in English.

We were both concerned. I silently asked God to help us. I was not sure what to expect. We walked across a bridge to another part of the city. We did not recognize anything. Then Nathan saw the Pizza Hut logo on a sign off in the distance. We walked to the building.

We were amazed. It was a regular Pizza Hut. We walked inside, and the workers spoke English. We ate some pizza and then Nathan used the Pizza Hut logo on the map to navigate back to our hotel. It felt so good to be warm inside the Pizza Hut. The Pizza Hut was amazing because Nathan and I had eaten at a Pizza Hut in every country we visited. We laughed about that on our way to the hotel.

the next morning, we took the train back to Finland. In Finland, we spent one night in a hotel and then took a flight back to California.

Trip To Las Vegas With Jessica

In 1994, Jessica and I planned a trip to Las Vegas. Jessica was a sophomore at San Diego State at the time. I drove to San Diego to meet Jessica before going to Las Vegas. We stayed in a hotel on the Las Vegas Strip.

Although I frequently gambled in Las Vegas when I was in the Marine Corps, I had not ventured since. Our purpose was to visit the city and see shows, not spend time in casinos.

However, Jessica and I wanted to see a costly show. I did not have enough money to cover the cost of the show and support the rest of the trip. I was nervous about it. I did not want to discuss it with Jessica, but I needed her to understand.

I thought about it for quite a while. Then that night while I began to sleep, I processed an idea. I calculated how much money I needed to pay for the show and still have enough money for the rest of the trip. I decided this one time to risk $100 on the blackjack table and either lose the $100 or raise the money we needed.

I discussed the plan with Jessica, and we proceeded to the casino. When I was in the Marine Corps, I sometimes flew to Nellis Airforce Base near Las Vegas on a Friday night and gambled all night, then flew home the next morning. It helped me get my flight time, and I enjoyed the casino. I always came close to breaking even for the night, which meant my entertainment was free. When I went off active duty, I never had any interest in gambling.

Jessica and I went to the casino. I purchased $100 worth of chips. We went to a blackjack table and began playing. Jessica watched. I lost the first two hands. Then I won two-thirds of the next ten hands.

Within an hour, we had won our goal. We left the table, cashed in the chips. We were happy that we had enough money to go to the show.

I realize this plan was not consistent with my Christian faith, but I did use my strong feelings to quit when we reached our goal. I wanted Jessica to understand possessing money itself was not essential and could be very destructive. However, when you want or need to do something that requires payment, it is good to be resourceful and honestly obtain the money necessary. I never wanted to worship money like an idol.

That evening we went to the show. We had a terrific experience. Both of us enjoyed the entire event. I was happy I had the opportunity to spend this time with Jessica. From the time I left her mother, I spent much less time alone with Jessica than I did with Nathan. I always went to her when I had serious questions about all my children. Jessica is brilliant and has excellent judgment.

Early the next morning, we both felt an energetic vibration. Back then, no one had cell phones. I had one for work but did not use it for personal calls.

We turned on the television and saw there was an earthquake near my house in Santa Clarita, California. The center of the quake was in Northridge, California. Nathan and his friend Jeff were staying at my home. We could see that the earthquake destroyed several of the houses in our neighborhood. I called the house, but the phone wasn't working. Jessica and I immediately checked out of the hotel and began to drive back to my home. When we reached the highway toward Palmdale, the police had blocked traffic and would not allow anyone to drive toward Santa Clarita.

Jessica and I were both terrified. We had no idea if Nathan and Jeff were alright or even alive. Luckily, I knew the area very well. I drove to side roads and worked our way toward the house.

When we finally arrived, the house was empty. There was a lot of damage, but the roof was still there, and most of the walls were in place. The quake destroyed the dishes and breakable items. The worst thing was that Nathan and Jeff were not there. Jessica and I hoped that was good news. We had no idea where to look for them. Finally, we found a message that gave the address where they were.

Jessica and I both were so happy when we saw them. It was challenging to get food, but the neighbors were cooking all their food because there was no electricity for the refrigerator. The food would spoil if not prepared.

Later that afternoon, Jessica and I left my house for San Diego so Jessica could return to school. The city closed all the main freeways near my house due to the damage. We managed to find a way to get past Los Angeles and Orange County. Then we were able to take significant highways back to San Diego.

Although this trip had tragedy, I did feel close to Jessica the entire time. She was so mature for her age. The experience was much better because of her. I did not discuss my prayers with her, but she knew how I felt. As with Nathan, I was so grateful that I was able to spend time together with Jessica, even though the trip was cut short.

Every time I think about that trip, I feel this special feeling for Jessica. She was so supportive the entire time. She was supportive when I did not have enough money for the show. She was supportive when we first knew about the earthquake. She was helpful when we tried to find Nathan and Jeff. God blessed me with all of my children.

Trip to Australia & New Zealand With Nathan

The last trip Nathan and I took together was in 2003. We spent three days in Sydney, Australia and two weeks in New Zealand. We did not hike or camp in Sydney. Sydney reminded me of San Francisco. It had buildings with beautiful architecture. The hills were almost as steep. The bridges across the bay were spectacular.

Sydney Opera House

The three days went so fast. Sydney is a city that welcomes people. There was so much to see. I hope we will go back and see other parts of Australia.

Nathan Looking at the Bay in Sydney

After the third day, we flew to Auckland, New Zealand. Auckland is on the North Island. We spent one day in Auckland and then flew to Christ Church in the South Island.

We spent one day in Christ Church enjoying the city. People were friendly, like in Sydney. We enjoyed seeing the city, but we were anxious to go to the southern tip of the South Island to begin our hiking.

We took a bus to Queenstown, which was at the southern tip of the South Island. Queenstown is a beautiful little town with a vast lake next to a mountain. Several hiking trails originated in Queenstown. We took three of those hikes during our ten days in Queenstown. We had a favorite restaurant for dinner called The Cow. We also watched a movie at a local movie theater. The town had about five streets. It also had boat rides on the lake. We went to the lake one afternoon.

The Cow Restaurant

The hiking trails were beautiful. The first one took us through the area where Steven Spielberg filmed "The Lord of the Rings". It was so beautiful. Each trail had kitchens and bunkhouses spaced throughout the trail so each night we cooked our food in a kitchen, and we slept in bunk beds. In the evenings we were able to spend time with other people from all around the world.

Nathan Crossing a Canyon

Fifth Near-Death Experience

We were near the top of a mountain when we began our hike one morning. The trail went alongside the edge of the cliff. As we made one turn, I slipped and began to fall. There were no trees at that elevation. It was a little over 5,000 feet to the bottom, which was rocks and dirt. Both Nathan and I thought I was on my way down. I managed to grab one small bush with my left hand. That one small bush was the only item insight. Nathan helped me off the cliff and back onto the trail. I had difficulty walking because I had strained my left leg.

I hiked the rest of the day, but the pain was severe. When we arrived at the next bunkhouse, I was so relieved. I thanked God for saving me. There was no explanation for one small bush to be within reaching distance.

That night I knew someone was taking care of me. I thanked God for everything. It felt so good to know I could make a mistake, and someone would be watching me. I know it will be part of God's plan for me to die someday, but until that day, I am so grateful for all the help and support.

Seeing Beautiful New Zealand

During a boat trip the next day, we saw mountains, waterfalls, and birds. We both enjoyed the boat. It felt good not to have to walk and still see the beautiful sights.

Nathan On the Boat

The next morning, we took a plane to Auckland, New Zealand. From Auckland, we flew back home.

Nathan Walking Toward Our Plane

The New Zealand trip was the last major trip I took with Nathan. I am grateful we were able to experience this time together. I frequently remember the trip fondly. It has been sixteen years, and I still remember so many details. It helped me feel close to Nathan. Sometimes God sends us messages, and we do not recognize them. I am happy I did understand the signal to spend one on one time with Nathan.

CHAPTER 9

WORKING THE BUSINESS

Changing the Leadership

By January of 1980, the business did not generate enough revenue to support Jim Ray or Bob Decker. Both accepted other jobs when they left the Marine Corps. I had a few customers, so I continued to run the business. For a while, Jim Ray and Bob Decker continued to help during off-hours.

I hired a software developer recommended by the local college. He was excellent; he had design and development skills. He made the modifications needed for Oakley and two other customers.

Then I met Mark Hilles. He responded to an ad. I hired him to help with sales and administration in the office. He became a very close friend for many years

We worked so hard to make the business grow but did not make a lot of progress. At that time, there was still no software distribution. There were a few computer stores, but they did not sell software.

I thought about closing the business. I prayed several times, asking for guidance. Then, just when things were becoming complicated, my former commanding officer from the Marine Corps called me.

Selling the Software – New Adventure

In early 1984, my former commander asked how the business was going. I told him we were breaking even, but there had been no growth during the past year. The software development was outstanding. We had a robust accounting system and a Customer Relationship Management (CRM) application (it was called Lead Management at that time).

We had several customers who were good references. The challenge was marketing. The only thing we did was advertise in the two computer journals that existed at that time, and I made phone calls.

My former commanding officer told me he had recently completed consulting with Security Pacific Bank. He indicated he was close to an executive there that wanted to talk with me about our software.

I was shocked that only one week after I prayed for guidance on whether to close the business, an executive from the fifth-largest bank in the United States wanted to talk with me.

I met with the executive. The discussion went very well. It seemed the technology portion of the bank was under new leadership, and they wanted to start backing technology-related companies.

I was fascinated by the discussion. After a few meetings, we reached an agreement. Security Pacific Bank would purchase all rights to my software for both applications. I would become a full-time executive for Security Pacific Bank. My position was Chief Operating Officer for a new company they formed called Security Pacific Computer Solutions.

The company would support all departments of the Security Pacific Bank and all the customers of the Security Pacific Bank (over 30,000 business clients). Later the company was chartered under Security Pacific State Bank so they could sell non-banking services to all companies.

The products we sold were computer training and the CRM application. I had significant experience with computer application training, so I worked with staff to create the courseware.

I taught the classes for the first two months, then trained instructors as I developed more courses.

The CRM Product I Developed

I Am Teaching a Class

The new Security Pacific Bank Company was very profitable immediately. I had two offices, one in downtown Los Angeles and one in San Francisco.

Later we added a third office in Orange County. It was an extraordinary situation for me. The bank paid me a high salary, I had a company car with a car phone (unusual at that time), and I had a large staff of highly educated professionals. I was treated well by the other executives. It was a big challenge to start the business and grow the revenue to a substantial profit.

My Office in Los Angeles

The president of the Security Pacific Bank at the time was George Moody. I developed a relationship with him because he needed help with his personal computer. George Moody was a strong Christian. Later, he left the bank to become president of the American Red Cross.

George Moody was also a good friend of President Reagan. During the 1984 Olympic Games in Los Angeles, President Regan had lunch with George Moody in the executive dining room.

I developed relationships with many large corporations who supported the bank, including IBM, which was the most prominent company. Security Pacific Bank was IBM's largest customer in California. I worked closely with IBM to help them with their customers. I spoke at several conferences in support of IBM.

I learned from IBM about selling to large corporations. At the time, they were the number one technology company in the world.

When IBM introduced a new mainframe system, they invited me to New York to view the ceremony.

I was surprised there were still a few IBM executives I knew from when I was in the Marine Corps.

A Plaque IBM Gave Me

Everything went well at Security Pacific Bank. The concept I learned when I played for the Southern California football team, to be a team player, worked exceptionally well at Security Pacific Bank. I developed relationships with several other entities, such as the Security Pacific Trust Company. Everything was good, but I felt like I did in the Marine Corps when I was not allowed to have friendships with the enlisted personnel.

Again, I had everything I wanted. The challenge was the politics at the bank seemed to be more important than the staff or the customers. I was there for four years. I was able to help many people develop their careers. However, after four years, I had accomplished everything I could to help the people around me. I was not sure why, but I had to leave the bank.

I prayed about the situation. This time I knew the condition was no longer suitable for me. I was not sure what to do. I prayed some more.

The leadership of the bank changed which helped me make the decision. Again, it was an answer to my prayers. The new leadership decided to close all the non-banking companies. Closing non-banking companies meant that Security Pacific Computer Solutions would be shut down. The bank allowed me to purchase my software. In 1986 I started a new company called Pyramid Software. I hired the brother of my original software developer. and began selling the software. Mark Hilles, whom I hired several years earlier, continued to work for me (I hired him at Security Pacific Bank as well). He had been with me for eight years. He helped me with all the non-development activities. We started selling software right away.

Pyramid Software Office

The company was profitable, but a stock market crash resulted in the depletion of investment capital and the growth the next few years was slow.

CHAPTER 10

FAMILY RESTRUCTURE

Nathan Moves to Live with Me

After Nathan and I went on the first hiking trip, he did feel better about himself. In December of 1988, Nathan thought he had too many friends that were bad for him. He called them losers. It was almost impossible for him to make positive changes to his life. He told his mother he wanted to come to live with me. His mother called me and let me know that she supported the move. Of course, I loved Nathan, but I was living in an apartment, running a business, and was unsure how to raise a child.

I prayed slowly about this one. I realized I wanted to be there for Nathan and give him anything he needed. I talked to him. I told him I was not a babysitter; he would have to make his bed and do his laundry.

By December of that year, his mother called me and said Nathan wanted to come to live with me. She repeated what Nathan told me, that he had friends that were bad for him, and he needed a new start.

I was very nervous, but I was also excited about living with Nathan. I went to get him at the beginning of his Christmas break from school. I could tell Nathan was nervous as well. He did not know anyone in Orange County, where I lived.

We went to school for the first day after Christmas break. After the first day of school, Nathan rode his bicycle to school. After school, he rode his bike home and then walked across the street to my office.

After a few days, he adjusted to the routine. He made friends with Jeff (the friend who was with us during the trip to Europe). Nathan improved immediately. I did not have any of the challenges with him his mother had. I took him to the community church I attended in San Juan Capistrano. After church the first week, we went to the beach. I thanked God for helping me stay close to Nathan.

Nathan on the Beach After Church

Nathan adjusted to living in Orange County immediately. He did well in school, developed relationships with a few close friends, and seemed to be enjoying life. His mother was pleased that he adjusted well. She was worried about him.

I was doing well with Pyramid at the time, so I bought a large house (5 bedrooms, 3,200 square feet) in a community neighborhood with clubhouses and swimming pools. I tried to make it as workable as possible for Nathan.

Nathan Selecting a College

Five years later, Pyramid Software went out of business. I was working for a consulting firm during Nathan's senior year in high school. He was researching colleges to attend the next year.

At the consulting firm where I was working, one of the managers was using drugs during working hours. I also discovered he was selling drugs. I called the owner and told him about the situation. The owner decided not to let the manager go. He just wanted to talk to him.

When I went home that night, I thought about the situation the entire evening. I knew the owner's decision was not workable. My challenge was that Nathan was looking at colleges. I could not afford to live without an income. I was not sure what to do.

I prayed that night. By the end of the night, I realized I had to trust my faith. I resigned the next day. The owner offered me a job in another office as the manager of that office. I knew after not sleeping the previous night; the situation would not work for me. I resigned.

I prayed for help. Within a week, a company I was pursuing when I worked for a consulting firm called me. The company wanted to hire me as a consultant for two months, and they would pay for the first month upfront. I was amazed that I went from depression to happiness in less than a week.

Nathan left with his friend Jeff to visit California State University Stanislaus the next week. I felt so much better. This time I was more prepared than back in Paradise. I knew to not judge situations until after things settle. That concept worked for me so many times.

Both Nathan and Jeff applied to Stanislaus. I tried not to suggest which college because I did not wish to apply any pressure on Nathan. After a few weeks, Nathan received a letter stating there was an issue with his application. One of his English classes was not at the correct level. Nathan worked with them on the subject, but the school was not approving his admission.

I suggested we drive up to California State University at Chico. I always loved that school. It was only fifteen miles from Paradise. Nathan agreed to see it.

We made the trip to Chico and Nathan liked the school. After Nathan completed the application process, I called the school, and they accepted him during the call. Nathan was happy.

Everything worked again. I thought about every time things seemed to be going bad, but then with faith, after time passed, things work even better than I expected. Nathan did very well at Chico. Hewlett Packard had a program at Chico. Nathan was an accounting and information technology, double major. His relationship with Hewlett Packard helped him dramatically after he started his career.

My Relationship with Jessica

Before Jessica left for college, she lived with her mother. I only saw her on weekends and not every weekend. As my firstborn, she was always extraordinary. She would call me occasionally to let me know how things were going. She made sure I knew anything important about Nathan. Of course, during her high school years and beyond, she did not respond to me as affectionately as she did before I left her mother.

She always thought about Nathan. Sometimes she asked me to take him on local trips. She wanted him to have something to do that was special, like her birthday parties. She was right; I took Nathan on long one day trips to Ventura, Santa Barbara, Solvang, and the beach. We had great visits to local spots.

On another one of Jessica's birthdays, I took Jessica bowling for the afternoon. That was a lot of fun, and it was a chance to spend one on one time with Jessica.

When Jessica was in college, I only saw her a few times a year. She worked to earn money and worked very hard in school. Jessica was an accounting major and worked toward becoming a CPA. She met her future husband while attending college. Then she moved to

Georgia with plans to get married. Her future husband was Catholic, which made the wedding complicated. It did not matter to me because I always believed the relationship with Jesus was private, and the church was a place to worship and learn about how to live.

However, the Christian church was not happy about two non-members of their church having a wedding at the church. I flew out to Georgia and met with the pastor of the church. Jessica went with me. After the meeting, the pastor agreed to host the wedding.

The Front of the Church

Jessica had a beautiful wedding. I was so happy for her. She was so detailed with everything in her life, planning the wedding was something she could do well.

A lot of people attended the wedding, and all of them seemed to enjoy themselves.

Jessica did a fantastic job, and everyone appreciated both the wedding and the reception.

Jessica and Justin at the Reception

I thanked God; the pastor married Jessica in a Christian church. That meant a lot to me.

I was happy Jessica asked me to talk with the pastor. As I mentioned previously, I did not force my faith on any of my children. Jessica always seemed to know how I felt. I was grateful for that. I loved her so much.

A couple of years later, Jessica gave birth to a baby. Jessica and Justin (her husband) named the baby Jaden. I knew Jaden was exceptional from the beginning. She had to be unique because she was Jessica's child.

CHAPTER 11

CAREER CHANGES

Another Software Development Company

In 1993, I began working for a software development company. It was like the one I started with my two friends after leaving the Marine Corps. The company had a business system designed to support the gift and apparel industries. I met with the owner, and he hired me as their Vice President of Sales.

Sixth Near-Death Experience

While working for this company, I traveled to twenty trade shows per year. During one of the trade shows in Atlanta, Georgia, in 1995, I was attacked while walking back to the hotel at night. It was a dark area and initially I did not see the attacker. He put a knife to my back, but said he had a gun, and kept trying to reach for my wallet. I was moving to deny him access to my pocket. My ID and credit cards were separate from my money, which was in a money clip. We moved in a circle, and he yelled for me to give him my wallet. Of course, I had been through many experiences by this time, and I knew to stay calm. I told him I did not want to damage my suit so he must let go before I would give him any money. He kept trying to grab for my wallet. I told him in a firm voice to let go. He pulled the knife away from my back and yelled that I was crazy. He ran away. I felt a spiritual presence that night. I knew I was not alone.

Established with the New Company

I enjoyed working for the company. I was with that company for eight years. I did not have any conflicts with my faith as I did in the Marine Corps, Security Pacific Bank, and the consulting company. The owner was sincere and allowed me to run sales without interference.

The business went well. We were profitable every month while I was there. Most of our sales originated at trade shows. I attended two trade shows a month. During those trade shows, I met many of our customers. Meeting customers was essential to me because I learned about how they were using the software, and they became references for future sales. I would give select customers advance copies of new software releases and try to help them if I could. One of those customers was special. His name was Gary Harrison. He maintained a booth at some of the trade shows we attended. He had a profitable import business from China. We developed a friendship that still exists today.

After eight years, I disagreed with the owner of the company regarding the product we were selling. I told him I had to leave. We parted friends.

Gary Harrison, the customer I met at the trade show, sold his interest in his company and became the Vice President of Sales after I left. We remained friends.

Back to the Consulting Firm

I went back to work for the consulting firm in February 2000. That went very well.

During the time I worked at the consulting firm, I became very active in the Democratic Party. I became a regional director for the Los Angeles County Party. I met many people who would help me later.

CHAPTER 12

RUNNING FOR CONGRESS

Initial Campaign

In 2004 and 2006, I won the Democratic Primary for the 46th Congressional District. I took a leave of absence from the consulting firm and worked full time on the campaign.

Howard Dean Endorsed Me

I was proud to be one of Howard Dean's "Dean Dozen" when he was the leading candidate for President of the United States in 2004.

My friend, Gary Harrison, became my campaign manager after I won the primary. I won the primary with more votes than my three opponents combined. However, the general election was different. I was running in a Republican district and lost the election. I had several other vital endorsements, but I did not have enough support to overcome the incumbent Congressman who had been in office for sixteen years.

Campaign Leadership Change – Big Mistake

One big mistake I made was that Governor Howard Dean suggested I hire a person from the Dean for President-California Campaign. I talked with Gary Harrison about it. Gary thought it might be a good move.

It was a terrible decision. Gary did not know politics, but I knew many people who did. Gary was excellent with technology and marketing. He was also great at meeting people. Gary managed the development of a website for the campaign that was far superior to other candidate websites. Within two weeks, I regretted the move and had to live with it. I did not listen to my prayer responses this time, and it probably cost me. I was very fortunate Gary and I remained friends.

General Westly Clark Endorses Me

Governor Bill Richardson Endorses Me

It was helpful to have widespread endorsement, but the dedicated volunteers are what drove the campaign. The Democratic clubs and labor unions provided the most help.

I did an event for the Women's National Democratic Club in Washington, DC. This club was a key club for Democrats all over the country.

Women's National Democratic Club in Washington DC

I met several key people from Washington during the event. I also ran in the Marine Corps Marathon while I was there. It was my fourth marathon.

Marine Corps Marathon

Twenty-six miles was a long run, but it felt good to finish. I ran the same race back when I was in the Marine Corps thirty years earlier. Of course, my finish time for this race was over an hour slower than the first one.

Campaign Office

We set up on office in downtown Long Beach to support the campaign. We had plenty of literature, yard signs, and volunteers to promote campaign events.

We also had plenty of volunteers who worked specific territories presenting information, brochures, yard signs, and pins. I had hundreds of volunteers from all areas within the district. Since the region was one third Los Angeles County and two-thirds Orange County, I worked with both county Democratic parties very hard. I also worked with most of the labor unions.

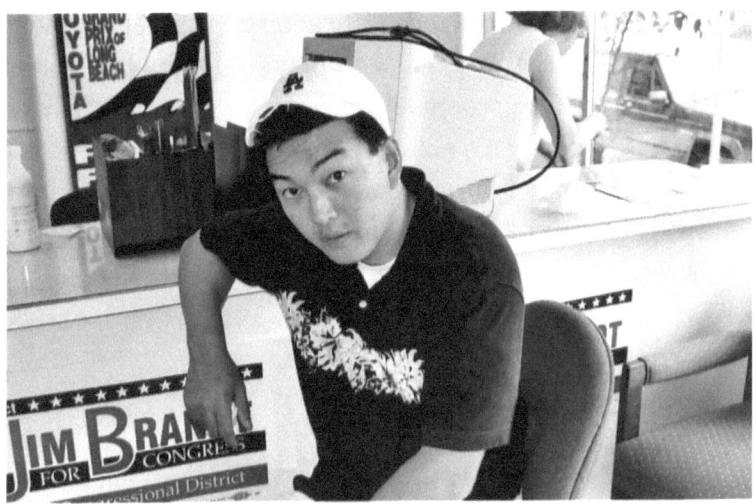

One of the Volunteers

During the campaign party on election night, many of my closest friends and supporters attended including my son Nathan.

Election Night with My Friend Gary Harrison

I felt very depressed that night because of the loss. I thought about the mistakes I made and decided to run a second time. Unfortunately, the results were similar. I spent a lot of time thinking about it. The party wanted me to run for office in a Democratic party district where there was an excellent chance to win.

I prayed about it but realized political office was not my end goal; it was a step along the way. As with playing football, becoming a pilot in the Marine Corps, being an executive at a national bank, and creating my own company, politics was not the place for me. I grew from it, but God's plan for me was to reach people. I could not do that and still be part of the government. It was a great experience, but I was ready to move to the next step.

CHAPTER 13

CHARITY NALZARO

Initial Introduction

B ack in 2009, I was celebrating New Year's Eve at Gary Harrison's house. Gary's mother-in-law, Elda, showed me a picture from Facebook. The image was Charity Nalzaro. Charity was beautiful. I was impressed but was not interested in finding someone. I had been unmarried for over twenty years and was independent. Also, the fact Charity was in the Philippines made things difficult.

Started with Interprise Solutions

In January of 2011, Gary approached me about joining his company, Interprise Software Solutions (later changed to Connected Business). I traveled to the Philippines with Gary back in 2005 to help with some of the planning for the company. I met many of the developers while in the Philippines. I was always impressed with Gary. I left the consulting firm one week later and began working with Interprise Software Solutions.

Charity was the Administration and Human Resources Manager for Interprise Solutions. During my first company trip to the Philippines, my plane arrived several hours before I could check into the hotel. I called the administration office, and Charity answered the call. I told her about the hotel, and she suggested I go to the company office. Charity said I could stay in her office until it was time to check into the hotel.

When I met her at her office, I immediately realized she was the same woman Elda had shown me two years earlier. She was so beautiful, and she had a great personality.

I did not say anything to her about seeing her picture earlier. After I returned home, Gary asked me if I was interested in Charity. I told him I was not looking for anyone, but I liked her. He asked me several times to ask her out on a date.

I knew there was something special about her, but I was happy living a single lifestyle. After a little time passed, I decided to ask her to dinner during my next trip to the Philippines. She said she would meet me for dinner.

I had no idea how much this date would change my life. We met at an Italian restaurant in one of the malls. As soon as we sat down to eat, I knew she was special. She was beautiful, articulate, and independent.

Charity

Charity let me know right away that she was a Christian. She mentioned that she attended the Seventh Day Adventist Church. I knew very little about that church. As I mentioned earlier, when I lived in Paradise, our church had services at the Paradise Seventh Day Adventist Church. However, I did not know anything about the Seventh Day Adventist Church.

My family taught me the church is not essential, it is the personal relationship with Jesus that matters. Therefore, I was not concerned about which Christian church Charity attended.

Meeting Charity's Family

After two years of spending time with Charity in the Philippines (four times a year), Charity arranged a trip for us to go together to her family's house. Her family lives in General Santos, which is a two-hour flight from Manila.

We had a terrific trip. I was able to spend time with Charity's family. Most notable was the time I spent with her father. He and I met alone. He explained the essential beliefs of the Seventh Day Adventist Church. The only idea I had to think about was regarding the Sabbath (worshiping on Saturday and keeping that day holy). He was very understanding. All he asked was that I would not interfere with Charity honoring her beliefs. I had no issue with that. I felt terrific about the entire conversation. I could tell the family had strong faith in God.

Charity with Her Family

Everyone was so lovely to me the entire weekend. During that trip, I realized I was ready to share my life. I was not mature enough during my first marriage to contribute enough to make the marriage successful. I decided I was mature enough for this one.

Charity's Father and Me

That weekend was special. Charity's family made me feel welcome. I did attend church with them and found it engaging.

Wedding Plans

Within a year after the visit with Charity's family, we planned another trip that included significant time with her family. I felt Charity was right for me, like God had brought us together. I knew she would help me improve my life.

It felt good to spend time with her family again. We also spent time alone. During part of the trip, we went to Davao. I always wanted to visit the Crocodile Farm there. Charity took me. I enjoyed the time with her. I held a small crocodile.

It was shortly after this trip that we made plans to get married. I knew this was the right decision for me. Every time I thought about Charity and God, it felt good. Our relationship was strong.

I immediately filed the paperwork for a fiancé visa. As soon as my paperwork was approved, Charity met with the US Embassy and completed her requirements, so the United States government issued the visa within a couple of weeks.

I Liked the Crocodile

Wedding in America

Charity arrived in American in January of 2015. The visa required a legal marriage within six months of Charity coming.

My parents were in their eighties at the time. My mother was staying in a senior care home, and my father lived at their home. We planned a small wedding near my father's house. Some of my relatives attended.

It was a special ceremony even though it was just in a local restaurant. I was happy my mother and father were there. My father was in the Philippines during World War II. He loved the Philippines and was delighted when he learned about Charity. He liked her from the first time he met her.

My sister Edna had a license to perform wedding ceremonies, so she performed the ceremony. Edna and her husband Bill made all the arrangements with the family and the restaurant. My Aunt Sharon was there. She was always special to me.

Wedding Party for the First Wedding

After the wedding ceremony, we had the reception at the same restaurant. Everyone had a great time. It was nice that with very little notice, my relatives traveled to be there.

We stayed at my father's house on the first night after the wedding. I was surprised everything went so well. That night I thanked God for the biggest event of my life since my children were born.

Wedding in the Philippines

We scheduled a second wedding in the Philippines. Charity did all the planning and most of the preparation. Charity flew to the Philippines four months before the wedding so she could manage the process.

Charity did an excellent job of using all the resources she had; considering there were well over 100 guests. Charity chose a superb venue. The wedding ceremony was on a beautiful grass outdoor facility with many bridesmaids and groomsmen.

Charity has an extensive family. Some of her family members drove eighteen hours to be there for the wedding. One of her family members had car challenges and still made it for the event. I was impressed with how large her family was and how much they care for each other.

The wedding ceremony was beautiful. The pastor was good, and all the children were delightful. We both loved the entire event.

The reception was in a beautiful building beside the ceremony's grass facility. The dinner was great, and it was good to meet more of Charity's family members in person. The entire event was fantastic.

I felt very close to God during the ceremony and very close to Charity's family during the reception. Everyone was so nice.

That night I thanked God. I knew Charity was perfect for me and my faith in God. All was well.

Charity and I at the Reception

Charity and I with Her Immediate Family

Charity's immediate family inlcudes her sisters, Sharon and Lilly, with Fritz (Sharon's husband) and Vohn (Lilly's son), Charity's brother JM and his wife Sheila with their two children (Ashley and JJ), and Charity's mother and father. The photographer took the picture inside the reception area.

Beautiful Charity During Our Second Wedding

Me Trying to Look My Best

Charity Adjusting to America

Charity is very independent. After she stayed in America for a few weeks, she learned the bus and train schedule. She had friends and relatives who lived near our house and some that lived in other states. I could see she needed to learn to drive and get her driver's license. Within six months, she accomplished something she had not done in the Philippines. She had her driver's license.

My sister Edna and her husband Bill offered to sell us their Honda Civic at a low price. Thanks to the help of Bill and Edna, Charity was completely independent. That made me very happy. I knew how close Charity is to her family and friends. She needed to have the freedom to travel where she wanted to go.

Within a short time, she began working as a caregiver. Now she not only was independent, but she was contributing to the family income as well.

Charity worked very hard in maintaining the house. She rearranged all the furniture and kept the house very clean. She also took care of the outside. She watered the plants, planted new flowers, and pulled weeds. I was amazed. Of course, I had to do everything before Charity, but I did not work nearly as hard as she did. I knew right away; she was even better than I expected. I knew I couldn't find someone so perfect. I knew God helped me. I am so blessed.

Charity's Parents Came to Stay with Us

Charity's mother and father came to stay with us about six months after the wedding. I believe her father had never traveled out of the Philippines. Her mother had a good position with the Seventh Day Adventist Conference and did go to some other countries.

It was beautiful to host Charity's parents. Charity took them on several trips. I was amazed because Charity only had her driver's license for a few months. She took them all over Southern California.

Then she drove them to San Francisco. That was amazing. They visited all the main sites. Then she drove them to Las Vegas. I was so happy to see her entertain her family. Family is so vital to Charity.

Her mother and father attended the local Seventh Day Adventist Church. They were able to meet our good friends there.

Then we drove to my sister Edna's house and stayed there for a weekend. That weekend went well.

By the end of their stay, Charity's parents were able to get a good feel for America. It was great to see them enjoy themselves.

CHAPTER 14

A NEW CHURCH

Locating a Church

I knew Charity would wish to go to the Seventh Day Adventist Church, so I found the location of a few of them before Charity's arrival. She attended one that was only two miles from our house.

After only attending a couple of weeks, she had already established a few friendships. We met one family for lunch on a Sunday. We all had a perfect time.

Attending the Seventh Day Adventist Church

I began attending the church shortly after Charity had decided this church was a good fit for her. Attending the Seventh Day Adventist Church was a significant step for me because before, I only attended traditional Christian churches that had Sunday as their holy day.

Adjusting to the change from Sunday to Saturday was difficult for me. Right away, I started attending the Sabbath School on Saturday mornings before the worship service.

It was good. I am not sure if all the Seventh Day Adventist Sabbath Schools operate the same way, but I benefited from this one. The leader of the group was James Barber. He has a strict Seventh Day Adventist background, but he was not judgmental. The class was interactive, so questions and comments from the group were common. It was good that the Seventh Day Adventist Church published the lessons and distributed them worldwide. The readings provided a systematic study plan that had specific objectives from week to week

I benefited from the lessons right away. There was one lesson during my first month that focused on behavior. The reading suggested not to overreact when things happened; like when you are driving on the freeway, and someone abruptly drives in front of you. Another example was when you drop something from the refrigerator, and it falls on the floor.

In both cases, you should ignore the anger. In the case on the freeway, it is better to give the driver some room and ignore the situation. It is not worth the stress when you honk the horn, yell, or make a gesture. Your health and your overall mood are more important than correcting the other driver. The same is true with the example of dropping something from the refrigerator onto the floor. It is not a big deal. It usually only takes a couple of minutes to clean the floor, and you forget about it.

I began to apply the lessons to work. Many times, customers would call me with what I thought were unreasonable requests. I would respond negatively and create challenges for the customer and me. When I applied the message from the Sabbath School, the problems resolved with much less stress and the customers were happy. The extra time it took to handle the situation correctly was well worth the result of a satisfied customer.

I do not mean I would do whatever the customer wanted, but I would not assume the customer was wrong every time. I would show them the respect of listening to their situation, and I would think about the situation from their point of view.

I felt a difference almost immediately. I also applied the concept to fellow workers and our channel partners who resell our software. I found that everyone has some positive thoughts to contribute. When I would assume everything was negative from specific people, it caused stress, and I missed some useful information.

Within months my relationships with friends, workers, and customers improved dramatically. I believe it had a positive impact on my health.

The Sabbath School focused on specific people in the Bible or events each quarter. The lessons applied to our daily lives. Now I have attended for more than four years, and I learn something new each week.

Although the church Charity and I attend is tiny, we both feel direct benefits from the experience. We have hosted many events at our house and felt good about all of them. It is beautiful when you can feel positive changes in your life.

Pastor Mu's Easter Message

The messages during the worship services have been helpful for me as well. The pastor, Filemu T. Filemu, we call him Pastor Mu, has delivered several sermons that impacted my life. He gave one specific sermon during the Easter weekend in 2017.

Of course, I have heard dozens of sermons about Easter. Pastor Mu's was different. Pastor Mu talked about what Jesus did on the day between the Crucifixion and the Resurrection. Pastor Mu spoke about how Jesus rested for a day after the Crucifixion. Pastor Mu explained how vital the rest was. He linked the message from the original creation when God rested on the seventh day to the Fourth Commandment when God told the enslaved Hebrews to rest on the seventh day.

I was fascinated by the sermon. I did some checking on the internet about working and resting. All the credible information I found from scientific sources indicated the human body needed rest at least once a week, preferably twice a week, to maintain good health. I was amazed.

Before that Sermon, I had run a minimum of 30 minutes (usually a lot more) every day for almost fourteen years. I did not go one day during that time without running. I immediately stopped running on

Saturdays to honor the Sabbath, and because I learned it was good for my health.

A Dream About Running

Shortly after changing my running routine, I had a dream. In the dream, I ran a marathon. I ran four marathons in my life. The last marathon I ran was twelve years before the dream. I did not believe I could run anywhere near the miles it would take to train for a marathon.

About a week later, I had a second dream with the same theme; I was running a marathon. I believed it was a message like I had received in the past, so I thought about it.

I accessed the internet to search for marathon training schedules. I reviewed them and began using one. After four weeks, my running had improved dramatically.

Then I registered for the Los Angeles Marathon and began seriously training at the beginning of June. The marathon was the following March. I was amazed. Within two months, I was running five miles a day on Monday, Wednesday, and Friday. I was running ten miles a day on Tuesday and Thursday, and fifteen miles on Sunday.

I maintained this schedule for several months until January. January was the strength month. I ran ten kilometers (6.2 miles) on Monday, Wednesday, and Friday. I ran twelve miles on Tuesday and Thursday. I ran sixteen miles on Sunday.

I was prepared to run the marathon. Then in February, I became ill with pneumonia. I was so sick I could not run and had to miss the marathon. I prayed about this. I wondered why I became ill if God wanted me to run the marathon. Then I realized running the marathon did not matter; the lesson about rest and the value of the Sabbath was what mattered. I did not need to run the marathon; I needed to prove to myself I was still able to do it if I worked properly and, more importantly, rested properly by honoring the Sabbath.

Teaching Bible School

We scheduled a Bible Study class on Wednesday nights at church member's houses. Several weeks later, Charity and I hosted the study. We enjoyed the fellowship of the group. I taught a few of the lessons.

One subject I taught was the Sermon on the Mount. As I mentioned earlier, that is my favorite passage in the Bible. I learned so much when preparing for the sessions. I applied many of the teachings to my life both at church and at home.

I created materials like those I created for customers at work during our training sessions. Creating the materials helped me understand many of the topics.

Preparing the Sermon on the Mount lessons and studying the lessons from the Sabbath School had an impact on my interaction with other people. At work, I did my best not to be judgmental and listen to the other person. There are a couple of people I did not respect. After preparing the lesson for the Sermon on the Mount, I had a different view of those two people. I began to see more value in their positions. I felt better about work in general.

I also learned from the Sermon on the Mount lessons that you should not allow disputes with other people to continue without resolution. When there is a dispute, you should address the other person involved, and you and the other person should settle it without talking to additional people.

I mentioned a close friend earlier in this book. His name is Mark Hilles. He was a very close friend who helped me in all my business efforts for more than twenty-five years. When I started my campaign for Congress, he was accommodating. Shortly after, we had a dispute regarding money. He left and returned to Oregon. I was so involved with the campaign; I did not contact him after he left. Later I discovered he was right; he did not owe me any money. I still did not try to reach him.

After going through the lessons of the Sermon on the Mount, I tried to reach him immediately. I found an address for him via the internet. I sent him a thoughtful letter. A few days later his brother called and told me he read my letter to Mark. He said Mark died three months earlier from cancer.

I was devastated. I felt awful for what I had done. Mark was a great friend. If I had followed the message from Jesus, Mark would know I was thinking about him and that he was a great friend. I pray for Mark every day. I will never get over this loss. I understand people must learn the message from Jesus as early as possible. We should all apply these teachings to our daily lives. We will all benefit from the results.

The lessons caused me to think about leaving Paradise, playing football, the Marine Corps, Security Pacific Bank, and many other events. I realized the concept I learned the day I left Paradise, "working for the team", applied to everything I do. When we do what we can to help others, it will improve our lives. Helping people is also true of a company, a church, a community, a state, a country, and the world.

I wish it did not take me more than sixty years to understand that by helping others, I will help myself.

I also learned from the Sermon on the Mount that I should keep the interaction between the person I am helping and me confidential. I never thought about it, but I realized it was true. If you brag about assisting others, it can cause negative things to happen. Your objective should be to help the other person, not improve your image.

Becoming a Church Member

After attending the Seventh Day Adventist Church for over three years, I decided to join the church. I did not wish to be baptized again because I was baptized with my sister Edna when I was sixteen, and it was special. It was important to me not to repeat that experience. The church accepted me, and I became a member.

I was still not sure the holy day is Saturday or some of the other rules of the church, but I prayed to God and made the agreement that I would honor Saturday as the Sabbath.

It felt terrific to become a member. I did not make that decision lightly, but it added meaning to my life. Charity was the reason I went to that church, but the improvement in my life was the reason I joined the church. I do believe the members of the church work for the team.

CHAPTER 15

MY PARENTS PASS AWAY

My Mother Passes

My mother was always there for my sister Edna and me. She always put us first. She wanted to be a part of everything we did. She worked very hard and did her best to make things better for us.

During the last two years of her life, she was very ill. She lived in a nursing home most of that time. Every time I visited her, I felt so sorry for her. She was so good for others. I wish I had done more to let her know how much she meant to my sister Edna and me.

My mother called me the day she died. I still do not know how she found my work phone number. She never called me at work in the past. We had a loving conversation. She seemed to remember much more than the previous discussions I had with her. I wished her well. Then later that day, my sister Edna called me to let me know my mother was gone.

We had a celebration of life ceremony with a few family members and a few guests. The service went fine, but I was so sad. She did so much for others, and she did have good relationships with many people. She had a personality that was offensive at times. I always miss her. She is constantly in my prayers.

My Father Passes

My father was the best person I ever knew. He helped everyone, regardless of who they were. My entire life, I remember him working to make things better for others.

About two months after my mother died, my father's health began to have challenges. He had healthcare workers staying with him in the last couple of months. He was still nice to everyone but had difficulties concentrating on anything. I called him on his last day. He told me it was time to pull the plug. I was so worried. Later that day, my sister Edna called me and told me he died.

We had just had a big birthday party for him one week earlier. There were over fifty people at the party. Even more, people came to his Celebration of Life Ceremony. I was one of the main speakers. It was good to have the chance to tell everyone about all the things I knew he did for others.

He even completed all the arrangements for his passing before his death. He made everything workable for my sister and me. My sister Edna and her husband Bill did all the work for the will, trust, and all the assets. I felt bad they had to do all that work. Charity and I lived so far away that it was difficult for us to be there regularly.

I was full of grief about both of my parents. There was nothing I could do except pray for them. I always think about them.

CHAPTER 16

FINAL THOUGHTS

I have a few expectations for this book. First, that my children read the book and give thought to how my faith in God has affected my life and theirs.

There were significant events in this book that dramatically affected my life. Several times I was driven to make a decision that was not the one I thought would benefit me. Every time I prayed for guidance, it led to a conclusion that helped me over time.

I wish when I was young, I understood how prayer affected decisions. I wanted to make football my career, but I chose another direction. I loved flying in the Marine Corps and thought a career would be fantastic, but I chose another path. I felt a position at Security Pacific Bank would meet all my dreams, but I chose another direction. I always wanted to be in politics, but when the party had a district for me to pursue, I chose another course. In each of those examples, I trusted my feelings and made decisions I thought were contrary to my best interest.

Now, looking back on those events, I see there was a plan for me, and I needed to have those experiences.

I hope some people will read this book and see the importance of their faith at a much earlier age than I did.

All the life-changing decisions I made were important, but when my first wife told me about her challenges with Nathan, the initial decision to take him hiking was the one that had the most significant impact on me. After praying several times, the image of taking him on a hike came to me. That decision lead to all the trips I had with my children. I did not feel helpless after that first hiking trip.

It was the New Life Seventh Day Adventist Church that helped me understand all the events covered in this book. The church was so open to discussing all my questions. I realized a person may be positive about a thought and later see things differently. The church accepted me and helped me apply scripture from the Bible to my life.

I deliberately did not refer to any specific Bible scriptures because I want this book to be about an ordinary man's faith. I do not interpret scripture, but I do have life experiences that relate to what church taught me.

Now I reached another decision point in my life. I believe I am ready to make a full-time effort to become a witness to how my faith in God has enriched my life. I realize the plan from the beginning led to this point. I am not a leader in the church, and I am not pursuing politics. My method goes beyond any specific title. I understand what the scripture has done for me, but I am not qualified to tell others what to believe. I can devote time and energy to let others know about my experience.

I am qualified to talk about my faith. I am a witness to God, and I will find a way in our current world to communicate my experience.

I want to thank the many members of the New Life Seventh Day Adventist Church who allowed me to grow with them. My father was my most excellent role model, and I think he would have liked my church. He taught me that the church you attend is not as important as your faith in God, but participating in the church helps you grow your faith and show respect for God.

I am ready to make the next move in my life.